Psalms Of My Heart

Christine Browning

RED TENT LIVING PRESS

Published by Red Tent Living
6523 Rose Arbour Avenue, Kalamazoo, MI 49009

Second printing, September 2016

Library of Congress Cataloguing-in-Publication Data

Browning, Christine.
      Psalms of My Heart/ Christine Browning.—1st ed.
      ISBN: 978-0-692-76601-9
      1. Devotional—Christianity. I. Title.

Printed in the United States of America
Set in Berthold Baskerville Book - Regular and Italic, Avalon, and Great Vibes
Layout by Wendalyn Park, Mi Print Works

Dedication

This book is dedicated to my grandchildren

Sam,

Emma,

and Sera

that you may come to fully know

the God revealed in the encounters written here.

He is our future and our hope.

I love you,

Grammy

Acknowledgements

"Thank you" rolls so easily off the tongue it often does not carry the weight of gratitude intended. Hearers often dismiss the depth of the words – the emotion behind the breath it takes to produce them. "Thank you" in the context of this little book coming to fruition is penned with much emotion, tears of gratitude, and heart-felt appreciation for the multitude of individuals who have contributed to this work. It feels dangerous and dismissing to try to name all to whom I am grateful for the production of this work – but I will name some, knowing I will unintentionally forget to name others.

To my friends, Karen Dixon and Eve Sherwood, who have read, advised, and encouraged me to dream into reality the 2nd edition of *Psalms of My Heart*.

To Tracy Johnson and Katy Johnson who believed in the work enough to take on its production. Their suggestions, encouragement, eye for detail, and extended kindness provided a safe space for me to dream and create.

To Allison Johnson for the stunning watercolor painting that became the cover for this work. Her sensitivity and artful expression beautifully capture my heart in whimsical color and form.

To Red Tent Living for opening new opportunities to explore places in my soul, space to write and share my story, and for their belief in the goodness of this work.

To Open Hearts Ministry, the organization that first introduced me to the possibility of healing from a life of trauma; at my first encounter with Open Hearts at a Survivors of Abuse Leadership Training Seminar (SALTS) in New Braunfels, TX in February 2006, I knew I had come home to a family where I was heard, seen, and loved – and to Katie Taylor who invited me to attend something I had no idea would change my life.

To Dr. Dan Allender, The Allender Center, Recovery Week, and the many good folks connected with Dan's work. Through all these venues I have experienced the goodness Dan's life and work bring to the deeply wounded, providing tools to fight back against the enemy's assault on faith, hope, and love.

To Dr. Richard Hipps, a pastor who allowed his own encounters with deep trauma and loss to produce a deep passion for God and a heart of kindness for others. Richard helped restore my belief that there are good pastors in this world who truly love God and lead others with integrity and grace.

To my children, Tom, Matthew, and Kristie, who have seen the worst and best of me and loved me still. Their navigation through the dark days and their courage today as they face their own need for healing brings me deep sorrow, repentance, and great joy.

To my husband with whom I have walked much of this earthy sojourn – we know the "secrets of the fire swamp." God has been more real in us and helped heal our love more in the last 10 years than in any of the previous 35. I am so thankful for our love story and look forward with joy to the years ahead.

To my colleagues, students, and friends at Milligan College who encourage me to be the best I can be and consistently call me to more. In particular, to Dr. Susan Higgins, who read through the manuscript and provided invaluable feedback and encouragement.

And to the God who sees, hears, and answers – for His great faithfulness to pursue me, call me to His side, whisper words of love to me, dance with me, and take me to new heights always, always leading me with tenderness and divine intention. *"Behold what manner of love the Father has bestowed on us, that we should be called the children of God!"* (1 John 3:1)

Endorsements:

"*The Psalms resonate in us because they intersect the cry of our soul with the desire of our heart. Our inner world needs words, especially in the midst of heartache. The Psalms also are meant to be prayed. We use the words of struggle and confidence to articulate what might remain dormant in us. They are also meant to prompt us to write verse to voice our deepest desires. Christine Browning has offered us a sweet gift of her psalms that were written and prayed through deep trauma. They echo not only the Psalms but as well the war of hope in our heart. Her poetic prayers invite us further into the mystery of how God redeems. He meets us in our pain and triumphs with us in our faith. Christine's life has known dark and hideous harm, and it is reflected in not only the pain but also in the creation of beauty. Read this great gift not only for comfort but as well to prompt you to write your heart.*" - Dan B. Allender, Ph.D., Professor of Counseling Psychology and Founding President, The Seattle School of Theology and Psychology

My dear friend and colleague, Dr. Christine Browning, writes about the pieces of trauma and loss that don't seem to fit together and perhaps never will. Entering her story through beautiful, challenging bone-honest poetry and prose will help you appreciate the fact that you are not alone in your suffering nor are you alone in your thoughts and feelings. Stories are powerful. Stories hold our world together. Without stories we remain isolated and vulnerable. Enter her story and find your own. I pray this book will offer you a spiritual perspective on what is happening to you, or has happened to you, one that is both biblical and life tested. - Dr. Richard Hipps, Senior Pastor, Trinity Baptist Church, Cordova, TN

Psalms of My Heart is Christine's invitation for you to discover your story through the eyes of one who has searched the heart of God and found the beauty of her own. Christine's prose and poetry draw you into her story of abuse, neglect and abandonment to a place of redemption. She is a poignant writer, one who will touch your heart deeply. - Mary Jane Hamilton, Author Living on Empty, Living in Gratitude

Psalms Of My Heart

Christine Browning

RED
TENT
LIVING

KALAMAZOO, MICHIGAN

Forward
Psalms of My Heart

It is such an honor to recommend this lovely journal of one woman's journey into places she never should have been, with people who knew better and didn't care about her heart. Christine's story is unique, as are all of ours. As she dares to let us walk with her into hard times and also the good times, we can find hope and encouragement for our own journeys, because there are some similarities. I have heard hundreds of stories and each time I want to say, "How did you make it?"

For thirty years I have been involved in small group work with men and women and I feel we are on holy ground when we hear each story. So much so that sometimes, I take off my shoes to show respect. Listening from our hearts is a gift we give to one another. As we read *Psalms of My Heart* and listen to the heart of this courageous woman, we can be encouraged to ask the Lord to help us find someone safe to hear our stories, enter our realties as a wounded person, and get healthy, truthful feedback.

The value of entering this story is that our own becomes enlightened. I was reminded how important it is for grandmas, and great-grandmas, to keep telling the story of Jesus to each generation. Christine's "Gram" was bedridden. And she did what she knew to do. She was a safe place for a child who had no one to see her with eyes of love and concern for her soul. I also know how important it is to respond to someone's secrets and pain. I want to say to Christine, "I am so glad you found the therapist who told you that your abuser should be in jail. I agree. You are a brilliant writer, a tenderhearted warrior, and a very, very good woman."

I am touched by her love affair with the Lord Jesus and the psalms, hymns, laments, and praise with their raw honestly. She makes me want to be more intimate with Him. This book is a "go-to" for a daily reminder of the ebb and flow of relationship with Him. We all need hope and help along the way. When you read and reread this book, use it devotionally and mark the pages with your own thoughts. There is room on the pages for you. You will be encouraged to relate to Jesus in a new way and will wish you could live next door to someone like this woman who has shown what redemption looks like.

Some people say to me, how do you listen to all those stories? Doesn't it depress you? Yes it did, until…I began to see how the Lord redeems the lives of

His people. He is using victims of abuse to turnaround and give help to others. The struggle to overcome is the very process that equips us; relationships with safe people, new ideas and ways of thinking and relating, counselors, pastors who have looked at their own lives, books, The Book, small groups, good healthy churches, and openness with others all are a part of the healing process. Writing and journaling are also a part of the healing journey. *"Let the redeemed of the Lord say so, whom He has redeemed from the hand of the adversary."* Psalm 107:2 Thanks, Christine. I am barefoot and cheering you on.

Sandy Burdick
Ministry Founder
Open Hearts Ministry

Introduction

"The basic premise of religion– that if you live a good life, things will go well for you– is wrong. Jesus was the most morally upright person who ever lived, yet He had a life filled with the experience of poverty, rejection, injustice, and even torture."

Timothy Keller

The original *Psalms of My Heart* was born of despair.

At twenty, I was a new believer living in a new town (Memphis, TN) with a new family (my father, step-mother, and her five children). Five very short years later, I was a wife and the mother of three children, the oldest being four years old. I knew my husband three months before we married. He was freshly home from the unpopular Vietnam War, having served twenty-four months in the Marines stationed near the demilitarized zone in Quang Tri.

As a young wife and mother of three, I lived a very solitary existence. My husband worked eighty hour weeks and was gone from home most of the time – even working overtime hours on weekends. Much of my time was spent mothering, attending church functions, or being alone.

I became a Christian two months before my husband and I married. A lifetime of trauma, abuse, terror, and chaos was the backdrop of my introduction to Christianity. The truth is the fallout from the abuse one suffers in childhood does not suddenly disappear at the moment of salvation. Oh, there is newness of life. Yes, there is forgiveness, and the prison doors swing widely open. The table is set, and manna is provided. But. The journey requires a community that offers feet to walk into the chaos of the past, ears to listen, and hearts to stand with; pray; and accompany one as she examines and grieves a lifetime of terror. The childhood survivor – newly born – must be invited to grieve all the horror from which she has been extricated. The cross precedes the resurrection. The disciples experienced deep sorrow over the death of hope before there was great rejoicing over Jesus' triumph from the grave. There are scenes from my childhood you will read here – scenes where evil came for me, sought to destroy me, was relentless in its bid for me…but I thought all that would suddenly disappear when I became a Christian. I thought my life would finally turn "right side up."

Often the church re-abuses survivors of childhood violence by preaching a gospel that does not address the need to honestly look at the damage endured and begin the necessary grieving process that accompanies one's healing. It is a journey. Statistically speaking, abuse is a momentary act of evil that carries a resulting lifetime of consequence. Patterns of relating are engrained from one's early years where necessary survival behaviors were learned. These patterns must be identified, grieved, and surrendered. Change is difficult. Trust – a mainstay of the believer – is a nearly impossible concept for a survivor of childhood violence to grasp. It feels treacherous to extend trust to anyone beyond the self.

Unfortunately, the invitation to examine and grieve my childhood harm did not occur until I was fifty-five, thirty-three years after my conversion. Prior to that life-saving invitation, exploitation, victimization, and sinister harm found its repeated assault on my young, vulnerable, lonely, needy life. Perpetrators can smell vulnerability. They exist on a diet of the naïve and unprotected. And, in this vulnerable posture, I was easy prey for a seasoned predator. Capitalizing on my lingering feelings of being abandoned and alone, the enemy moved in for the kill.

My main perpetrator after my conversion was a man of considerable stature in the community, someone I saw every Sunday. Important. Well-respected. Kind – at first – but masterfully manipulative. Winding his web of deception around my trauma-infested, needy heart, he eventually gained my admiration. He groomed me slowly to test and ensure my devotion. Then, with calculated intent, he threatened to kill my children if I did not submit to his perversions. The threats were backed one terrifying afternoon when, brandishing a loaded gun, he warned, "no one ever crosses me and lives."

And I submitted so he would not carry out his threat.

In the aftermath of his abuse – in desperation and with serious consideration of suicide – I told my husband of the man's evil pursuit. There was misunderstanding to address and persecution to endure – mostly from our Christian community. Only a few dear friends stood with us as the uncovering of this man's history in other churches revealed a trail of abuse that stretched back years and included many women with past histories that resembled mine.

This is the point at which the first *Psalm* was written – penned – prayed. The first book began as words written in my journals during early morning prayers to the God who sees, hears, and answers. These times with God were my lifeline. I literally could not breathe without first coming to Him for the moment-by-moment promises I needed to move forward. Over the next fourteen years,

God opened doors for the writings to be shared in a local newspaper as a devotional column. Patrons of the paper wrote letters of identification with the words and eventually asked that a book of the published writings be gathered into a collection, which emerged as the first edition of *Psalms of My Heart.*

It has not been an easy journey of recovery from the various forms of abuse I have experienced. By its very definition, no journey is easy. After many long years struggling alone, God brought me to a community of believers who were also survivors of childhood abuse – Open Hearts Ministry. Through their ministry to the wounded, I began to see my story housed within the greater story – His story – the gospel. Because of this ministry of healing, I now know that my story is one story of redemption within God's grander story of Calvary love. My association with Open Hearts Ministry and Grace Groups also introduced me to Red Tent Living and the good work of inviting women to more. I was invited – not only to take a place at the table – but as one who is honored as an equal member of a community of women sharing life, love, story, and hope. I was invited to life.

> *"At the end of history the whole earth has become the Garden of God again. Death and decay and suffering are gone. . . . Jesus will make the world our perfect home again. We will no longer be living 'east of Eden,' always wandering and never arriving. We will come, and the father will meet us and embrace us, and we will be brought into the feast."* - Timothy Keller

God does not waste anything. He makes beauty out of ashes. He whispers how and where to take the "next right step." As you sift through the ashes of my story, I invite you to also see the beauty. And as my story invites you to look honestly and deeply at the ashes of your own story, I pray you will begin to ask Him to show you the beauty He has written there. Don't rush the journey. If we sidestep the cross and hurry to the resurrection – we do not see the full glory of it. Take time to sift through the ashes. Take time to grieve. And as you begin to see places of redemption – take time to rejoice.

My prayer as I write these words of introduction is that, as you travel through the pages of this little book, you will know hope and help as you journey through this passage of your life with the God who sees, the God who hears, and the God who answers. May you know His presence with you as you read, pray, and consider His ways. May you also hear God sing over you as you identify and grieve the places where you have known harm. And may you find comfort on your journey, knowing there are others willing to walk into the chaos of your story with you, sit with you as you grieve, walk with you as you take the "next right steps" of your journey and begin to heal. Thank you, from the depth of my heart, for taking time to read the words written here; may they bring comfort to you along your way.

Many blessings to you,
Christine

Psalms of Orientation – Salvation

Salvation, n. | sal•va•tion | \sal'vāSHən\.

deliverance from the power and effects of sin; the agent or means that effects salvation; liberation from ignorance or illusion; preservation from destruction or failure; deliverance from danger or difficulty – through faith in the Lord Jesus Christ, the spotless "Lamb of God who takes away the sin of the world." (John 1:29)

New Life

I was lost and rejected.
You sought me.
You bought with Your own blood
my soul.
I was struggling to make life
worth living.
You asked me to give You
control.
I had nothing of worth
left to bring You.
"Nothing's needed,"
You whispered to me.
"You've been purchased,
redeemed and atoned for
by My death
on Mt. Calvary."
I gave only a dead,
sinful heart, Lord.
You buried the guilt
of the past.
You shattered the pain
of the present.
I found peace and contentment
at last.

2 Corinthians 5:17 *Therefore, if anyone is in Christ, he is a new creation. The old has passed away; behold the new has come.*

At Calvary

His robe of glory
laid aside
He came to walk for me
the dark, despairing
rugged path;
the road to Calvary.

He held creation
in His hand
His word brought forth
the world.
Then clothed in
flesh's humanity,
our sin on Him
was hurled.

He had the right of
conquering King
to blast all to the grave.
But humbly on a
shameful cross
His blood for me
He gave.

Oh, lest I lose
the wonder
of Your depth of love
for me,
Dear God, remind me
fresh today
of You
at Calvary.

Luke 23:46-48 *Then Jesus, calling out with a loud voice, said, "Father into your hand I commit my spirit!" And having said this he breathed his last. Now when the centurion saw what had taken place, he praised God saying, "Certainly, this man was innocent!" And all the crowds that had assembled for this spectacle, when they saw what had taken place returned home beating their breasts.*

Beholding Your Salvation

Lord,
In Psalm 91 You declare,
"I will let him behold my salvation."
That is what we do, Lord,
whenever we exchange
our way
for Yours.
We lay down the death of self
and put on the Life of Christ.
Help me so walk, Lord,
that I am continually,
in every circumstance,
beholding Your salvation.

Psalm 91:15, 16 *He will call upon Me, and I will answer him; I will be with him in trouble; I will rescue him and honor him. With long life I will satisfy him, and let him behold My salvation. (NAS)*

The Door

I was a poor lost little lamb
Without a shepherd or a fold.
The days were long and rugged,
the nights were dark and cold.

The hungry wolves oft followed me,
I fell in many a snare.
How desperately I needed
A Tender Shepherd's care.

While I was lost and wandering,
The Tender Shepherd came;
"Enter at the Door," He said,
"And you will know My Name."

Oh, praise the Shepherd of the fold
He is that blessed Door
that leads to joy abundant
and life forevermore!

John 10:9 *I am the door; by me if any man enter in, he shall be saved and shall go in and out and find pasture. (NAS)*

The Exchange

I was lost, confused, condemned.
I found the Way, the Truth, the Life.

My blinded eyes saw darkness,
You showed me the Light of the World.

I had searched so long for food,
You fed me the Bread of Life.

The world's way left me thirsty,
You poured me Living Water.

I brought nothing –
You gave Your all.

I Timothy 1:14 *The grace of our Lord was poured out on me abundantly, along with the faith and love that are in Christ Jesus. (NIV)*

Unmerited Benefits

I came to You
broken
dirty
covered with shame
my garments torn and filthy
reeking of sin.

You healed me
cleansed me
covered me with Your precious blood
gave me a robe of righteousness
and a sweet smell.

Thank You,
Precious Father,
for the unmerited benefits
of Your love.

Psalm 103:1-6 *Praise the Lord, O my soul; all my inmost being, praise his holy name. Praise the Lord, O my soul and forget not all his benefits—who forgives all your sins and heals all your diseases, who redeems your life from the pit and crowns you with love and compassion, who satisfies your desires with good things so that your youth is renewed like the eagles. (NIV)*

Faith

Where doubt prevails
confusion reigns…
When faith looks up
God sustains!
Have faith in God.

Mark 11:22 *"Have faith in God," Jesus said. (NIV)*

Love

Thank You
for showing me
how much You love me.
I searched a long time
in this world
for love
but only found poor imitations
emptiness
rejection
abuse and loss.
I never knew
Love
until I saw
Your love for me
at Calvary.

I John 4:10 *This is love; not that we loved God, but that he loved us and sent his Son as an atoning sacrifice for our sins. (NIV)*

Jesus in Me

My eyes were blinded
You made me see.

My lips were as poison
You bridled me.

My feet ran to mischief
and turned aside.

Your steps led me home,
My Heavenly Guide.

My heart was deceitful
and wicked and cold.

Your life brought light
to my desolate soul.

How fearful and empty
life would be,

If You had not come
to live in me.

I Corinthians 6:11 *And that is what some of you were. But you were washed, you were sanctified, you were justified in the name of the Lord Jesus Christ and by the Spirit of our God. (NIV)*

God's Wisdom

Help me never
lean my faith
on the shoulder
of another man's philosophy,
but cling to
trust in
and die for
the clear, concise wisdom
of Your divine revelation.

I Corinthians 1:24b, 25 ... *Christ the power of God and the wisdom of God. Because the foolishness of God is wiser than men, and the weakness of God is stronger than men. (NAS)*

Fragrance

Father,
I pray that You
will continually
break open
my life
so that the
fragrance of
Your Spirit
can cleanse
and refresh me
from the stench
of my sin.

Psalm 51:17 *The sacrifices of God are a broken spirit; a broken and contrite heart, O God, you will not despise. (NIV)*

A Walking Epistle

Father,
Forgive me
for going into the darkness
of my past
and putting on
the garments of
death and defeat.
I will never
be an effective
walking epistle
without the
proper attire.

Ephesians 4:22-24 *Strip yourselves of your former nature – put off and discard your old unrenewed self – which characterized your previous manner of life and becomes corrupt through lusts and desires that spring from delusion; And be constantly renewed in the spirit of your mind – having a fresh, mental and spiritual attitude; And put on the new nature (the regenerate self) created in God's image, (Godlike) in true righteousness and holiness. (Amplified Bible)*

Windows of Wisdom

There are windows of wisdom
That I am looking through.
Each trial – each experience
Gives a glimpse of something new.

I've a loving Heavenly Father
Holding me up to the sill
Helping me to see more clearly
As I yield all to His will.

Come; look through these windows with me;
There is beauty to behold,
Silver blessings of obedience
And wisdom of pure gold.

Colossians 1:9 *For this reason also, since the day we heard of it, we have not ceased to pray for you and to ask that you may be filled with the knowledge of His will in all spiritual wisdom and understanding. (NAS)*

Make Me a Prism of Light

Father,
Like light through a prism
shine the light of Your Spirit
through me
and let the
colorful glow
of Your presence
permeate
my life.
Let those with whom I live
and work
and walk
and talk
see the abundant
diversity
and beauty
in the mighty spectrum
of Your love.

Ephesians 5:8 *For at one time you were darkness, but now you are light in the Lord Walk as children of light.*

A Fool's Belief

Father,
This morning, sitting at my
kitchen table
I can feel the
gentle morning breeze,
see the dew-kissed ground.
I hear the birds
singing sweet praises to You;
there is a rooster crowing,
a woodpecker already
busy at work
and in the distance
the faintest hooting of an owl.
The sky is a clear and boundless blue
stretching to eternity.
A sliver of the moon
is still visible
as the sun climbs.
My babes are sleeping,
breathing softly.
Matthew's thumb hangs loosely
from his little lip,
his blanket clutched tenderly
under his arm.
Everywhere I look, Father,
I see You
hear You
feel Your presence.
Only a fool could say,
"There is no God."

Psalm 53:1 *The fool has said in his heart, "There is no God." (NAS)*

Kept By the Power of His Love

Father,
I am so thankful
that all eternity
does not hang
on the thread of my belief.
I am thankful
that when I am
faithless
You remain
faithful still.
This is not an excuse
to live less than all for You.
But it is the
instrument
that unchains me
from the doctrine of
approval some preach.
It is Your kindness
that leads us to
repentance
and in that humble surrender
it is Your Spirit
enabling the
weakness and fear
of my flesh
that makes a difference
in this broken, ransomed life.

Lamentations 3:22, 23 *Because of the Lord's great love we are not consumed, for his compassions never fail. They are new every morning; great is your faithfulness. (NIV)*

His Little Lamb: A Hymn

Take me as a little lamb, Lord,
Helpless, needful as can be.
Shepherd, lead my every footstep
Till I safely rest in Thee.

Yes, the way seems dark and lonely,
Trial brings the thought to stray.
Bind me to Your loving heart, Lord;
Let me choose to cling, to stay.

Onward lead me in the battle;
Keep my eye upon the Son.
Faithful now, Lord, I would serve Thee.
Faithful till my journey's done.

Thou our Great Commander lead us,
Draw us ever near Your side.
Safe in Jesus, all victorious
May we rest and there abide.

John 10:14 *I am the good shepherd. I know my own and my own know me.*

I Belong to You

Father,
How comforting it is to
know with steadfast assurance
that I belong to
You.
Nothing – in any form
image
manifestation
or reality
can separate
my life
from Your
provision,
not only in this life,
but in the blessed life
to come.

Psalm 73:24 *You guide me with your counsel, and afterward you will take me into glory. (NIV)*

His Thoughts Toward Me

"How precious to me
are Your thoughts, O God!
How vast is the sum of them!"
I stand in awe
at the measure of Your love
poured out on me.
Before I was
ever formed,
You loved me.
Nothing in me was
hidden from You.
No darkness in me
or around me
can withstand the
brilliance of
Your consuming Light.
You beheld me
in my sin,
and loved me.
You drew me by Your Spirit,
heard my cry of desperation
cleansed me
and filled me
with new life.
Oh, Father,
thank You for Your life in me!
Live through me
to the uttermost
the moments,
days,
months,
and years
You have recorded in
Your plan for me.

Psalm 137:17 *How precious to me are your thoughts, O God! How vast is the sum of them! (NIV)*

A Father's Love

The dreaded call
every parent of a
teenage driver fears
came Wednesday afternoon
during a downpour of rain,
"Your daughter's been in an accident."
The moments between
that statement
and her voice on the line
seemed centuries.
"I'm okay mom, but the Blazer…"
My mind began to
calculate
possibilities still void of facts
(sometimes an active
imagination is an enemy)
As I drove to the site
her 16 years
flashed in precious moments
before me.
Never was there
anger at her deed…
only love
concern
understanding.
As I drove past the
twisted metal
felled light pole
and broken glass
my eyes flashed from
scene to search
for my child.
I parked and ran toward the crowd,
still searching.
At last I spied her
huddled in their midst.
I wrapped my arms around her

and squeezed
thankfulness expelling with each breath.
"Mom, look at the Blazer..."
she cried.
"Blazers can be replaced,
Kristie's can't,"
was my choked out response.
I thought of You, Father,
and of my countless mishaps,
how You love with a love
beyond understanding,
and I wept.

Jeremiah 31:3 *I have loved you with an everlasting love.*

No Condemnation

Father,
remind me
that You never speak
to my heart
in tones of condemnation—
but You
gently
tenderly
often firmly
nudge me to attention
with specific suggestions
and precise instructions.
With You
there is always
fresh hope
and a new beginning.

Romans 8:1 *There is therefore now no condemnation for those who are in Christ Jesus.*
(NAS)

Held in His Hand

Thank You
that my foot stands
in an even place
because I am held
in the unwavering
unfailing hand
of my Father.

Psalm 26:12a *My feet stand on level ground. (NIV)*

His Sheep Am I

There are so many voices
in the world.
So many advisors.
So many choices.
Thank You that
Your sheep can hear Your voice
and follow You –
the thief seeks to
confuse
steal
kill
and destroy
but we are held in the
hand of the Father –
secure
guarded and guided by
the Great Shepherd.

John 10:27-29 *My sheep hear my voice, and I know them and they follow me. I give them eternal life, and they will never perish, and no one will snatch them out of my hand. My Father, who has given them to me, is greater than all, and no one is able to snatch them out of the Father's hand.*

Tugs

You, Father,
are so aware of me
so interested
so concerned
that not even
my feeble
half-believing
tug on the hem of your garment
goes unnoticed.
Thank You for the
freedom
to tug
and know that I am
not only noticed
but welcomed
with forgiveness
and eternal love.

Mark 5:25-27, 34 *And there was a woman...who had suffered much under many physicians, and had spent all that she had, and was no better but rather grew worse. She had heard reports about Jesus and came up behind him and touched his garment. For she said, "If I even touch his garments, I will be made well." And he said to her, "Daughter, your faith has made you well; go in peace and be healed of your disease."*

Psalm 91

How precious to be
in the shelter of Thee
there is refuge in Your
fortress of love.

I'm covered, protected
by Your mighty wings,
I'm delivered with
grace from above.

I need never fear
the terror by night
nor the arrow
that flieth by day;

Neither evil nor plague
will come nigh unto me,
Your truth is my shield
and my stay.

Wherever I go,
though I tread upon lions,
Your angels
keep watch over me.

You will answer, assist,
deliver and honor;
You have shown
Your salvation to me.

(based on the actual Psalm 91)

Alpha & Omega

Father,
I praise You
that You are
Alpha and Omega
of all things.
Be the Alpha
the beginning
of my day.
Grant me the
fresh touch of Your Spirit
to carry me through
this vapor of time
and when I draw
my feet into bed
tonight
be the Omega
the glorious ending.
Lord, put a
perfect parenthesis
around each
moment and hour of this
portion of my pilgrimage
making my life
a sweet savor
of Christ to You.

Psalm 138:8 *The Lord will fulfill his purpose for me; your steadfast love, O Lord, endures forever. Do not forsake the work of your hands.*

God's Love

Father,
Your love is like the
ripples in a still pool of water.
They begin
with one
penetrating touch
and expand in
every-widening
circles
until they reach
from shore to shore.

I John 4:19 *We love, because He first loved us. (NAS)*

His Jewel

Father,
You live amidst
streets of pure gold,
jasper walls
pearly gates
a city garnished with
all manner of precious stones
sapphire
chalcedony
emeralds
sardonyx
sardius
chrysolite
beryl
topaz
amethyst –
and yet,
You call me
Your jewel!

Malachi 3:17 *"They shall be Mine," says the Lord of hosts, "On that day that I make them My jewels. And I will spare them as a man spares his own son who serves him."* *(NKJV)*

Sunrise/Sunset

Everywhere I look
I see traces
of my Heavenly Father's love.

In the sunrise
I see the dawning of His love
on my soul.

In the sunset
I see the beautiful glow
that illumines a life spent with Him.

With each new morning and evening
the God of all creation
puts the glow of His
unfailing love in the heavens
for all to see.

Genesis 1:14 *And God said, "Let there be lights in the expanse of the heavens to separate the day from the night."*

Love

Love in the Garden created
then clothed.
Left innocence bare
then covered sin;
and banished disobedience
from perfection.
But Love did not stop
with rebuke.
Love went on to
forgiveness and restoration.
Though by one man
sin
entered the world
and death by sin
so death passed upon
all men, for all have sinned.
Though through the
offence of one
many are dead
much more
the Grace of God and the
Gift of Grace
which is by ONE MAN
JESUS CHRIST
has abounded unto many.
He leads me in the paths of
righteousness
for His name's sake;
He restores my soul.
Love poured out His life
as that Gift of Grace
at Calvary.
And that same
Love
has arms outstretched
to welcome you.

Genesis 3; Romans 5:12; Psalm 23:3

Eternal Reminder

There is no need
for me to ever feel
forsaken or alone.
You cannot forget me.
You are eternally reminded of me.
I am engraved on the
palms of Your hands...

Isaiah 49:16(a) *Behold, I have engraved you on the palms of my hands...*

Eternal Need

Father,
as I walk out into the
world of eternal need
grant me a
heartbeat for their hurts
and an
ear for their troubles.
Cover me with the
Grace of Calvary
that I might
speak with the eternal concern
You have for
each problem
life
need.
Help me remember
I am not called to be their
answer.
I am called to point the way to
The Answer – Christ.

Luke 19:41 *And when he (Jesus) drew near and saw the city, he wept over it.*

Eternal Freedom

When our forefathers
first came
to America
they invited You –
we became
"One Nation Under God."
But today,
there are those
who would have You
thrown out of the country!
How my heart aches for America, Father,
when I think of the
multitudes
in our free nation
who have never experienced
the gift of Your
eternal freedom.

Proverbs 19:21 *Many are the plans in the mind of a man, but it is the purpose of the Lord that will stand.*

A Teacher's Prayer

Father,
a child
is a fragile possibility
in the hand of his teacher.
He can be
maimed or motivated
chided or challenged
shaken or secured
discouraged or directed.
Lord,
help me be
an instrument of grace
in the lives of the children
You have entrusted
to my care.

Proverbs 25:17 *A word fitly spoken is like apples of gold in a setting of silver.*

Fall

A time of reflection…
cool mornings
with cups of warm coffee
for chilly hands.
Steam rising from
country ponds.
Red glowing sunrises
and purple hued sunsets.
Pumpkin patches bloom
baled hay dots the landscape
and the foliage
explodes
with a glorious array of color
calling us to stop, look and
consider Your creation.
Football games
with bands
and cheerleaders
spread an excitement
across a parental crowd.
Books read best
when snuggled
in a comfortable chair
under an old afghan
and in the company of
an evening fire that
welcomes frosty toes.
Thank You, Lord,
for the beauty of
Your world.

Genesis 1:31(a) *And God saw all that he had made, and behold, it was very good.*
(NAS)

His Bounty

How thankful we ought to be
for the bounty of our God.
To those in darkness,
He is the Light of the World.
To the hungry,
He is the Bread of Life.
To the thirsty,
He gives Living Water.
To the lost,
He is the Way.
To the confused,
He is the Truth.
To those bound by death,
He is the Resurrection and the Life.
To those drowning in despair,
He is the True Vine.
To the shut out,
He is the Door;
And to those who have
come to Him through faith,
He is the Good Shepherd.
Oh, friend,
at His table
there is abundance of life
through the bounty
He offers to every man
in Jesus Christ.

The Gospel of John

Psalms of Disorientation – Lament

Lament, v. | la•ment | \lə'ment\.

Using words to frame the deep feelings and questions surrounding our loss; to feel or express sorrow; mourn, grieve, sorrow, wail; a profound or demonstrative expression of sorrow.

Lament

As I began to walk into the scenes of my story, my eyes opened to the "data," as Dan Allender calls it, that revealed descriptive details of abuse. And with the details, more of my story unfolded, opening more of the wound of my childhood, providing more reasons to grieve, and finding more of God's faithfulness at every turn.

Introduction to Psalms of Lament

What does your heart look like? What is the terrain of your heart? What are the textures, colors, smells? Does your heart have mountains? Walk around in it and describe it to me. When did that valley form – what mountain have you most often climbed? These are questions that were posed to me in different ways during a journey into the terrain of my heart. I was invited there by Dan Allender through his books, lectures, and experiences of small group learning at The Allender Center and Recovery Week. That work began to build upon what I had learned of my heart during my first attendance at *The Journey,* an Open Hearts Ministry function.

I have been struggling with writing my story for many years…actually I began writing it when I was very, very small, but it was written in tones too discordant for the human ear to hear and with words too confusing for the human hand to write. The words of my story are filled with chaos, violence, loneliness, and dark despair. Conversely, the words that form my story, now partially written, are also sprinkled with life-giving splashes of great joy, laughter, motherhood, companionship, mentoring, friendship, and love. As I read the list I smile, acknowledging the balance leans more toward joy than sorrow…funny how that goes so unnoticed to the shutdown heart.

The scenes of shame that entered my young, innocent heart began in the home of my Aunt Lola and Uncle Ed. My Uncle Ed was a predator who noted I was curious, largely ignored and unprotected, and that my young heart longed for connection.

When I was four years old, my family lived in a duplex in Berkley, CA. Uncle Ed and Aunt Lola lived in the upstairs apartment; my family lived downstairs. I stayed with my uncle and aunt while my father was at work and my sisters were at school. Although my mother did not work, she was in the last trimester of her pregnancy with my brother, so I was often sent upstairs to stay with my aunt and uncle, even after my brother was born. My first vivid memories are steeped in that apartment.

Uncle Ed had a study off the main living room area in the upstairs apartment. I remember it as a stuffy room that was soaked in the smell of pipe tobacco and alcohol. The wall that opened to the main living room was a french door; the three additional walls that comprised the room were floor to ceiling dark mahogany bookcases with glass doors. On every inch of every shelf behind the glass bookcase doors were National Geographic magazines—a sea of yellow everywhere I looked. A large brocade divan, small oval coffee table, cherry secretary, and oriental rug strewn with newspapers filled the tiny room.

Uncle Ed first lured me into his study with a magazine that had pictures of natives with plates in their lips. It was fascinating and colorful and enticing— and the people were naked. The women had breasts that hung down to their waists and the men had firm naked butts. I had never seen anyone naked. I was soon on Uncle Ed's lap and, after we looked long at several of the pictures, he clutched me close to him with one hand while he gently fondled me with the other. The stubble of his beard was sharp and rough against my cheek, and he smelled like stale beer. When my mother found out I had been in the study with Uncle Ed—I guess I told her—she scolded me: "Christine Marie, don't you ever go into that room with that dirty old man ever again, do you hear me young lady?" Her comments filled me with shame. It was after that incident I remember my mother sing-songing a nursery rhyme to me whenever my behavior displeased her, which was often: "*There once was a girl with a pretty little curl right in the middle of her forehead* (this was enunciated with her index finger pressed firmly against my forehead); *and when she was good, she was very, very good but when she was bad, she was horrid*" (she would screw up her face into an awful scowl and remark sharply), "...and *you* Christine Marie are *HORRID!*"

I have been unsure whether or not to publish this book until both parents are dead. I have no desire to hurt my parents, to cause them any discomfort in their waning years. I would certainly not derive any joy from seeing them squirm away from the truth – and worse – I might invite a barrage of accusations and fury much like those I have spent many years trying to erase from my memoryscapes.

In *The Singer* (1984) Calvin Miller records his impressions of a risen Savior returning to visit a child He healed before His crucifixion. She is writhing in imagined agony, groping for her legs, "that had not suffered any loss for all her worry" (p. 141). Surprised by His sudden visitation on the "small mat that is her bed," the child springs up and dances with joy to see him then jumps to hug him with such force "it all but knocks him over!" (p. 141). A beautiful conversation ensues.

> **Child**: Oh, Singer—I was so afraid. I thought my legs would be as...
> **Singer**: Yours are far better than mine this morning.
> His hands and feet were barely recognizable. She who had cried for her own legs was overcome by real concern for his.
> **Child**: You healed mine! Heal your own. Please, Singer, make them well.
> **Singer**: They are well. There is no pain now.
> **Child**: But they are scarred and wounded. How can they be well?
> **Singer**: Earthmaker leaves the scars, for they preserve the memory of pain. He will leave my hands this way so men will not forget what it can cost to be a singer in a theater of hate.
> **Child**: But the word...the word they wrote upon your face is gone.
> **Singer**: It is, because Earthmaker cannot bear a lie. He could not let me wear the word for He is Truth. He knows no contradiction in himself. So learn this, my little friend, no man may burn a label into flesh and make it stay when heaven disagrees (pp.141, 142).

The nursery rhyme my mother recited to me shortly after my first encounter with Uncle Ed, was periodically repeated to me over several decades of my life. In fact, the last time my mother recited that rhyme to me I was in my 50's. The tape of its rhyme and message replayed whenever I experienced a moment of shame, whenever I disappointed – myself or others even in small ways – whenever I was in a position to be evaluated by others. Understanding that part of my story identified the origin of the nursery rhyme in my life and the ripping, tearing pain it has inflicted across the years. Even as a Christian, I felt my life useless – to myself, to others, and most certainly to God. The cries of lament written here come from the deeply buried places of shame that were born in my four-year-old heart. I read them now as desperate but beautiful cries to the God Who knows and loves me. I can trust Him with my pain, my wounds, my scars, and know with certainty that, "no man may burn a label into flesh and make it stay when heaven disagrees."

His Voice

I listened for You in the multitudes
I listened in groups of three.
I listened with the faith of others
but You did not speak to me.

I tuned my ear to theologians
Well-versed in theology.
I listened with my intellect
but You did not speak to me.

In the quiet of my chamber
I knelt humbly on bended knee
And asked with the heart of a trusting child
If You would speak to me.

"I can't be heard with the deafness
Of a humanistic ear.
I quietly call to the seeking heart
Who listens by faith to hear."

Hebrews 4:2 *For indeed we have had good news preached to us, just as they also, but the word they heard did not profit them, because it was not united by faith, in those who heard. (NAS)*

The Doubter

Father,
How can I
convince
the doubter
the skeptic
who try to
reason the
eternal things of Christ
with the intellectual mind
that the Light of Your Life
can only be seen
through the
eyes of faith?

Matthew 16:17 *And Jesus answered him, "Blessed are you, Simon Bar-Jonah! For flesh and blood has not revealed this to you, but my Father who is in heaven."*

Rebellion/Obedience

Rebellion is a
clenched fist
thrust in the face of God
closed to
His will
His way
in His time
for His purpose.

Obedience is an
open extended palm
into which
a loving Heavenly Father
can pour
His grace to endure
all things.
And with that same hand
of His yielded child
God can touch other lives.

Psalm 88:9 ...*Every day I call upon you, O Lord; I spread out my hands to you.*

Failure

Father,
How quickly we are drawn
into the lure of the world's
"harmless fun."
We go directly from
speaking a timely word
by Your Spirit's urging
to speaking a word
out of time and
out of the vain embarrassment
of wanting to be
"accepted."
We falsely convince ourselves
that by this friendly association
we can be used to show the
unsaved
that Christians are
"not so bad after all."

Proverbs 13:20 *Whoever walks with the wise becomes wise, but the companion of fools will suffer harm.*

On the Fence

Father,
I cannot
be a friend of the world
or speak the language
of the world
or love the things
of the world.
If I sit down
by the devil's fire,
I won't get warmed –
only burned,
and I will mar Your
reflection in me.
Help me take a
definite stand for You.
And, Father,
please help me
down
off this fence.

Matthew 6:24 *No one can serve two masters, for either he will hate the one and love the other, or he will be devoted to the one and despise the other. You cannot serve God and money.*

Glowing

Father,
Please help me place more
emphasis
on my inward glow
than on my
outward show.

2 Corinthians 4:6 *For God who said, "Let light shine out of darkness," has shone in our hearts to give the light of the knowledge of the glory of God in the face of Jesus Christ.*

The Full Flame

Father,
Touch the
spark
of Your Spirit
in my heart today
that it may grow
from the ember of obedience
to the full flame
of Your complete control –
and in that
flame
burn away any lingering
debris of self.

Proverbs 23:26 *My son, give me your heart, and let your eyes observe my ways.*

The Face of God

In Exodus 33:20 *God said, "no man can see me and live!"*

That is a hard statement. There is no room for compromise in it. To see the face of God brings death to self. When I truly humble myself before God, I am seeking His face. That glance, that gaze, that fixing of my eyes upon Him requires a death to the things in me that demand their own way. The humanity of Christ expressed it this way in Gethsemane, "Not my will, Father, but your will be done." I have to, then, ask myself, "Do I want to see the face of God? Am I willing to die to that thing He puts His finger on in my life, or do I love it more than 'seeing' Him?" When He does put His finger on it, I can no longer walk in the blindness of that disobedience. I must die to my desire to see things my way, or stumble in the darkness of my stubborn will, dimming still more His light upon my path.

Do you desire to see the face of God?

Desert Places

Father,
Thank You for the
desert places.
When my
breath is hot,
my throat is dry,
and my strength fails,
I reach out
with renewed
and intensified longing
for the thirst-quenching
soul-satisfying
Living Water.

And, Father,
forgive me
for forgetting
how sweet and refreshing
the Water is
when I am in the
green pastures
of a fertile field.

John 7:37-38 *If anyone thirsts, let him come to me and drink. Whoever believes in me, as the Scripture has said, "Out of his heart will flow rivers of living water."*

Fear

Father,
The Roman soldiers
set a seal
on the tomb
while the disciples
hid in fear
and forgot Your promise
to rise again.

Keep my mind and heart
fastened on Your promises
that I might not
hide in fear
but run and tell
the multitudes
of Your soon return.

John 20:19 *On the evening of that day, the first day of the week, the doors being locked where the disciples were for fear of the Jews, Jesus came and stood among them and said to them, "Peace be with you."*

Transformed

Father,
Help me not be
conformed
to the image of evil
by the pressures
of this world –
rather let me be
transformed
by Your indwelling power
daily.

Romans 12:2 *Do not be conformed to this world, but be transformed by the renewal of your mind, that by testing you may discern what is the will of God, what is good and acceptable and perfect.*

My Way

Oh Father,
I stand in arrogance
and out and out
rebellion
on the throne of my life
throwing things at You
to keep You away
keep Your voice quiet –
and You are
noticeably quiet.
All I can hear
is my own voice
loud
clamoring
whining
demanding my way –
screaming selfish and prideful
desires –
until I fall
in a frenzy of sin
at the foot of the cross.
I give You back
Your rightful authority
over my life
at the center
on the throne
of my heart.
I joyfully submit
to Your perfect provision
and Lordship.
I am weary of running
my life
my way.

Proverbs 16:25 *There is a way that seems right to a man, but its end is the way to death.*

Want List

"The Lord is my Shepherd,
I shall not want."
Lord, still the battle
rages
from time to time in me
with WANTS.
I want
forbidden physical pleasures
then You remind me
of the passing pleasure of
physical satisfaction
and the eternal satisfaction
of Your love.
I want
material possessions
(just **one** more thing?)
But You gently teach me
the futility of
holding on to things
that are passing away.
I want
Fame
world recognition
but You remind me
that those who have it
would be the first to tell me
how empty and temporary
fame is
hung on the thread
of human whim.
Success is not
me being known by man
but me being known by God
through Jesus Christ.

Psalm 23

The Little Lamb

Oh Father,
How much this little lamb
needs the green pastures,
still waters,
and paths of righteousness
of the Good Shepherd.
Teach me that my want list
has been fully satisfied
in You.

Psalm 23:1(a) *The Lord is my shepherd; I shall not want.*

Green Pastures

I was wondering today, Lord,
why do you MAKE me lie down
in green pastures?
Is it because
left to my own ways
I would not make the best
choices?
Could You know me so well
that You commandeer circumstances
to bring me into
the green pastures
I would otherwise not see?
Thank You, Father,
for the pastures of my past
once viewed as
barren and rotting.
A reflective glance
brings rich, green,
fertile insight
and a heart to see
the blessing of Your love.

Psalm 23:2(a) *He makes me lie down in green pastures.*

The Shade of a Huge Rock

Oh Lord,
In the dry desert dust of
self will
I lay crying over
circumstances of my own making,
failures to follow You.
My self effort left me
parched,
spent –
surrender was a welcome release.
Immediately Your forgiveness
refreshed
and set me in the shade of the
Rock that is higher than I.

Isaiah 31:1a, 2b *Behold, a king will reign in righteousness…like the shade of a great rock in a weary land.*

War

Father,
My imagination runs wild
like a madman hiding
an invisible assailant prowls in opposition.
I cower and strike at things
my mind's eye produces
things that don't exist
things that belittle and accuse others –
and me.
It is a distracting technique
of the enemy
sent to keep my mind occupied
with unseen buffeters
trivial temporal pursuit.
God help me keep my eyes
fixed on You.
This invisible battle is not fought
with earthly energy
or sensual strategy.
It is to be fought first
from a position of
total dependence and trust.
It is fought in
humility
with grace and certain aim
at every prosecuting oppressor.
I swing with wild sword slashing
cutting off ears.
You gently remind me to lay
earthly weapons down
and wield the certain sword
of Your Spirit,
shield of Faith held high
Helmet of Salvation
Breastplate of Righteousness
Girdle of Truth
Feet ready to go and tell

the Good News
with every cadenced breath
a continual Prayer
of commitment and conscious resolve to
"Stand still and see the Salvation
of the Lord on my behalf." (*Exodus 14:13; 2 Chronicles 20:17*)

Luke 22:48-51 *When those around him saw what was going to happen they said to him, "Lord, shall we strike with the sword?" And one of the them struck the servant of the high priest and cut off his right ear. But Jesus answered and said, "Permit even this." And he touched his ear and healed him. (NKJV)*

Throwing Stones

An immoral woman
was taken in the act of her sin
and thrown at the feet
of Jesus.
Her accusers were
bent on her destruction
sure of her penalty.
But Jesus spoke harshly to
their unworthy judgment
and in complete, redemptive
love
forgave her.
I was once flung in the dust
of my own depravity
at the Savior's feet,
touched and changed
by His forgiveness.
How then can I so quickly
join the howling mob
in condemnation of another?
Oh, Lord,
remind me
that I am nothing
aside from Your touch
and grant me the
compassion of Your grace
to extend my hand in love
with no hidden stones
in my heart.

I John 4:11 *Beloved, if God so loved us, we also ought to love one another.*

Prayer

Lord,
Teach me to pray.
I've been in a
well of hell
surrounded by
my idle thoughts
my wishing lists
and wants –
my own voice
deafeningly clear
no longer hears
Your whispers sweet
to love
to care
for others –
just blinding thought
of me
until I am sick to death
of me.
Lord,
teach me to pray.
Let food and thought
lose grip and care
till all my focus
everywhere
is others' needs
and praise of You.
Lord,
teach me to pray.

Psalm 34:15 *The eyes of the Lord are toward the righteous and his ears toward their cry.*

Surrender

Unbelief cannot stand before You.
In whatever form we flaunt it
or try to conceal it
Your Spirit will search it out
and with quiet reminder
nudge it to
our inescapable attention.
It becomes a
hindrance to
praise
worship
prayer
to any form of
communication
with You.
But made an offering,
release of self,
placed on the altar of God –
it is consumed
and the smoke of its
surrender
becomes a
sweet savor
of Christ to God.

Hebrews 12: 29 *For our God is a consuming fire. (NAS)*

Time Flurries

Thoughts reel
and confuse
time dances by
laughing at my
helplessness
in its fleeting pace.
Demands mount
filling each moment
with the pressure
of constant insistence
to be met
concluded
satisfied.
The stillness of Your voice
in the flurry of activity
and thought
is almost overlooked.
But I come
I kneel
I stop to listen
and in the ceasing to strive
against an unconquerable enemy
You flood in
with peace
assurance
rest
and hope.

Psalm 32:7 *You are a hiding place for me; you preserve me from trouble; you surround me with shouts of deliverance.*

A Promise Kept

Father,
You have said
"My thoughts are not
your thoughts.
Neither are your ways
My ways."
As I read Your word
I consider again
Mary,
visited by an angel
A virgin surrendered
to the love of her God;
her life an acceptable outpouring.
What thoughts fueled by fear raced through
her heart that lonely night?
Her prayer of praise
came later.
In my simple mind
I wonder, Lord,
if Mary struggled
with Your perfect plan for her,
as I do with Your
perfect plan for me.
Being pregnant before marriage
was not acceptable behavior
in Mary's culture.
Her entire
reputation
was laid on Your promise.
In the sure-ensuing rumors
and misunderstandings,
Mary stood firm in praise
and believed God.
When life ceases to be
sensible
and does not fit the mold

my own desires design,
help me trust Your ways,
and know Your plan IS perfect.

Luke 1:45 *And blessed is she who believed that there would be a fulfillment of what was spoken to her from the Lord.*

For Yang

A friend came by for some
conversation
friendship.
There is a thread of
deep respect that runs
between us.
He is someone I admire
and enjoy conversing with.
Unguardedly
my lips formed
careless words of
unintentional prejudice.
A flippant remark
that stung him like
a face slap.
The room and conversation
fell silent
as I struggled to recover
my composure
and his respect,
but his deep wound
hung in his glance
and he quickly left
the company of my
careless conversation.
Father of my deepest thoughts,
I give to You the
hidden prejudices of my heart.
Unearth them all
that I may not be an
open sepulcher
or white-washed stone –
clean without
but full of filth within.
Cleanse me from the
secret faults

that lay beneath the
surface of my life
yet linger
on the tip of my tongue.
I experienced
with fresh pain
the meaning of those words
today.

James 1:26 *If anyone thinks he is religious and does not bridle his tongue but deceives his heart, this person's religion is worthless.*

Outward Appearances

Father,
I am doing it again.
I have taken my eyes off
You
and put them on
ME.
My face in the mirror aging –
40!
Trips to the salon
hair color
nail polish
frantically trying to hide
years.
Why?
I have condescended to worshipping
creature
not Creator.
Oh Father,
Take my feet out of this
mire of self
and put them back on the
Rock.
You are the same
age to age.
You change not
and Your desire for my
happiness and peace
is the nurturing and
building up
of the inner woman of my heart.
This body began to decay
at birth.
Nothing can stop that –
dust WILL return to dust.
But Your Spirit in me is alive
Forevermore!

I Peter 3:3-4 *Do not let your adorning be external—the braiding of hair and the putting on of gold jewelry, or the clothing you wear—but let your adorning be the hidden person of the heart with the imperishable beauty of a gentle and quiet spirit, which in God's sight is very precious.*

Dead Men

We scratch
claw
and seek to get more.
We devour one another
in our attempt to climb
higher
on the material
corporate
political
even religious
ladder.
We discard food
while the poor starve.
We gather wardrobes
for moths
save whales
and fight for fur rights
while babies die
in back allies
and respectable abortion mills.
We have closed our eyes
to our own sin.
Instead we call it
"attitudes."
We laugh at
sitcoms that show
disrespect for father
and mother
and applaud their
mindless blasphemy
of God.
Oh, Lord,
that we would see You
again with clear eyes –
our soul stripped bare
before a Holy God.

That we might
fall at Your feet
as dead men
and pray for
forgiveness.
There is no hope
apart from You!

Revelation 1:17-18 *When I saw him, I fell at his feet as though dead. But he laid his right hand on me, saying, "Fear not, I am the first and the last, and the living one. I died, and behold I am alive forevermore, and I have the keys of Death and Hades."*

Proud Wrath

Proud wrath
screams at the children
puffs up
and separates friends.
It causes arguments
headaches
heartaches
and never resolves or heals
anything.

Proverbs 21:24 *Scoffer is the name of the arrogant, haughty man who acts with arrogant pride.*

The Real Enemy

So often I battle against
flesh and blood,
against the attitudes and actions of others.
Help me remember
that my warfare is not with
a society,
school of thought,
or an individual.
My foe is an
invisible enemy.
Satan.
And must be addressed with
supernatural power.
Thank You, Lord,
for being my
strength and shield,
for preparing me for battle,
for training my hands to war.
Thank You for the armor You
have provided for my protection
and for the promised provision
of a way to escape
each temptation.
Thank You, Father,
for the radiant reminder
that though we have
tribulation in this world,
we can be of good cheer
for You have
overcome the world!

Psalm 18:34; Ephesians 6:18-21; 1 Corinthians 10:13; John 16:33

Stained Glass Religion

I long for us to see You
outside the stained glass
the printed page
the sterile prayer.
I long for us to see You
with skin on
reaching to the
broken
the blind
the lost
the unkind.
Reaching, always reaching
past tradition and training
past organization and committee.
Reaching through
misunderstanding
division
and unbelief.
Down to the heart of man
with the heart of a man
and the hand of God.
Reaching
into the center of our
death
placing life
in all who welcome
Your touch.
Father, touch the church today.
We are singing
"I believe"
with our lips
while we march along in the death
of our organized
traditional
stained glass
unbelief.

Philippians 2:10-11 *...so that at the name of Jesus every knee should bow in heaven and on earth and under the earth, and every tongue confess that Jesus Christ is Lord, to the glory of God the Father.*

Our Refuge

Though sin's waters
rage about me,
though winds of
temptation roar,
though the dark clouds
of defeat
and discouragement
sweep o're,
there's a sweet
refreshing river
gently flowing in my soul.
There I find a quiet refuge
and a shelter from the cold.
There the Savior
bears my burden
as I yield all to His will.
There He takes me
in His loving arms
and whispers, "Peace be still."

Psalm 46:1 *God is our refuge and strength, a very present help in trouble.*

The Rock

Father,
I am so thankful
that You are
"The Rock that is higher than I."
When I am being tossed about
You are steadfast in Spirit.
When my faith wavers
and my heart is
overwhelmed,
when I am in despair,
I cry to You
and You lead me and lift me up
and hide me in the Rock.
Today, Father,
I am tossed about,
wavering
overwhelmed
in despair
and crying.
I am so thankful
I have You.

Psalm 61:2-3 *From the end of the earth I call to you when my heart is faint. Lead me to the rock that is higher than I, for you have been my refuge, a strong tower against the enemy.*

Jesus Wept

Today, Father,
it grieves me to see
so many
who ignore You.
Multitudes who mock
Your precious name
with only a breath
between them
and eternity.
They don't even notice
Your pierced hands
reaching out to them
in love,
longing for them
to accept Your gift
of eternal life.
No wonder
when You stood
looking out
over Jerusalem
You wept.

Luke 19:41 *And when he drew near and saw the city, he wept over it.*

A Needy People

In the midst of our
piety in religion
and wealth as a nation
we are spiritually bankrupt.
We skip off to church
with our oversized Bibles
to hide our lack of
hunger for You.
We raise one hand to pray
while the other
toyingly embraces
the claw of the demon messenger
sent to deliver our
besetting sin;
never really coming to grips
with our need before You.
Totally void of good
we rush home to feed our ego
with position
possession
and performance.
We hide the deep gaping
needs of our heart
in our own accomplishments.
Oh, God,
help us see
what a needy people
we are.

Isaiah 53:6 *All of us like sheep have gone astray; we have turned—every one—to his own way; and the Lord has laid on him the iniquity of us all.*

Mid Life

Lord,
I seem to be in transition
stepping out of the young married realm
into mid-life.
I have heard the sarcastic remarks about the
possible
crisis
of these years,
and I have laughed along with the rest.
But it has ceased to be funny
as I have entered the turmoil of
sifting through the deluge of my own
exaggerated expectations
to find and follow after You.
You alone are The Way,
The Truth and The Life.
As the ebb of time
creeps noticeably closer
to my middle years,
help me look back and
remember the God Who led me
out of Egypt (sin)
and into a land
flowing
with milk and honey (salvation).
You are the same
yesterday, today, forever,
and You alone know the
end from the beginning.
For the Christian,
You are not only the
beginning and end
You are also the in between.

Psalm 90:12 *So teach us to number our days that we may get a heart of wisdom.*

Seeking Through the Pain

Father,
I sought You
with a heart of pain
bitterness deafening
Your clear response.
I sought You again
with a heart of confusion
and bitterness
straining with increasing
difficulty,
listening for Your voice.
I sought You in anger
with a heart of confusion
and bitterness
demanding that You tell me
what to do.
In despair and anger
with a heart of confusion
and bitterness
I gave up in repentance
and You answered
with a cleansing hope
of forgiveness.
Oh, Father,
Thank You for calling
this wanderer
home.

Psalm 91:15 *When he calls to me, I will answer him; I will be with him in trouble; I will rescue him and honor him. With long life I will satisfy him and show him my salvation.*

Spiritual Surgery
A Psalm for my daughter.

Father,
As I watched
Kristie
wheeled off to surgery
this morning
I was aware
in a very small way
how much it hurts
You
when we undergo
spiritual surgery.
Though the surgery
is usually minor
and not
life-threatening,
You know
it will hurt
for a little while.
But You see beyond
the hurt
to our health
when the healing
is complete.

James 1:3 *For you know that the testing of Our faith produces steadfastness.*

Waiting

Father,
It seems I cry out to You
in my grief and distress
and only hear
silence.
I lean up to hear Your voice
I strain from reaching for You
yet You seem illusive
hiding Your face
silent.
I will stay long at the
brook of Living Water
to feel Your refreshing touch.
My throat is parched
My heart is all but dried up.
Tears no longer come
from my eyes.
Sleep flees from my tormented
fatigue
and still I wait to hear
from You.
Counselors advise me
friends pray
and wring their hands
to understand and be a help to me.
But my eye is on You, Lord,
and I will hope in You
though You remain silent.
I know You as the God Who
ponders
what is best for me.
Let me be content
to wait
for Your best.

Psalm 69:3 *I am weary with my crying out; my throat is parched, my eyes grow dim with waiting for my God.*

Thank You for Coming

Father,
Thank You for coming
this morning.
I was feeling
depressed and alone.
I don't know
my neighbors well yet,
the children are
at school,
and Tom is at work.
The house is too quiet.
I needed someone
to talk to,
and You always
make me feel better.
Thank You for coming!

Luke 24:32 *They said to each other, "Did not our hearts burn within us while he talked to us on the road, while he opened to us the Scriptures?"*

Squeezed

Father,
When I am
pressed in on every side,
when demands on my time
far outweigh my capacity
to accomplish,
and the enemy
seeks to destroy my confidence
in You;
quiet me
still me
permeate me
with Yourself
to such fullness
that when I am being
squeezed
all that will
exude from me
is You.

2 Corinthians 4:8(a) *We are hard pressed on every side, yet not crushed. (NKJV)*

The Storm

Father,
In the midst of
the storm at sea
tossing the
tiny fishing boat
in which Jesus slept,
the disciples
feared for their lives.
Awakening Christ
with cries of terror
He immediately
stilled the storm
revealing their
needless fear
and His Omnipotence
Sovereignty
in any situation
circumstance.
Oh, Lord,
let the storms come
and trouble my life
that the impurities
in the cargo of
my heart
will be made visible to my eyes.
Then give me
the courage and insight
to see You
in the fullness
of Your glorious deliverance
from every threatening storm
and say afresh in my spirit,
"What sort of man is this,
that even the winds and the sea obey him?"

Matthew 8:27 *And the man marveled saying, "What sort of man is this, that even winds and sea obey him?"*

Always Near

Though enemies lurk
and the thick black clouds
of despair
and defeat
hang over me
though evil intent presses me
to the ground,
I know You are always near
and You will
prevail.
You will bring
a cloudless morning
a golden dawn
and a new day.
Evil does not win.

Psalm 25:2-3 *O my God, in you I trust; let me not be put to shame; let not my enemies exult over me. Indeed, none who wait for you shall be put to shame; they shall be ashamed who are wantonly treacherous.*

Instant Pressure

There is an instant pressure
in pain
that reminds me to seek You.
There is an insistence
in persecution
that demands the comfort of
Your arms.
But there is a putting off
there is a
waiting to read
to pray
to seek Your face
when the crisis has passed
and the fear subsided.
Oh, Father,
forgive my tendency to be as Pharaoh.
Let me be instead
as a deer panting for
the water,
my soul longing always
after You.

Exodus 8:15 *But when Pharaoh saw that there was a respite, he hardened his heart and would not listen to them, as the Lord had said.*

Love is Blind

It must really be amusing
to You
to witness my tantrums
to observe
how much I feel I "deserve"
especially on those
worst self-pity days
when all the world
is against me.
I was feeling just that way
as I drove to work
one recent morning.
Even after I parked and walked to the building
I grumbled
rehearsing my woes to You
in rising and falling tones
of despair.
It was just before I turned
to catch the elevator
that I caught a glimpse of You
in them.
He was crippled.
She in a wheelchair.
He struggled hard against
the mismatched rhythm
of his body's movements and
the forward motion of her chair.
But he pushed,
his captive rider
jerked
with the cadence
of his handicap,
yet her face was lit up with a smile.
As he pushed
a glorious grin danced playfully
in his eyes
and across his lips.

They glanced briefly at me
and then they were gone
around the corner of the corridor,
carrying their gift of gladness
past other grumblers.
"Love," it is sometimes said
"is blind."
Their love was the love
of Calvary –
reaching beyond fault
to need.
I gladly deposited both
grumbling and long face
somewhere on that elevator
between the first
and fourth floors
and spent a wonderful
heart-soaring day
giving thanks.

Exodus 16:8(c) ... *Your grumbling is not against us but against the Lord.*

Giving Up

Father,
The world is full of
giver-uppers.
We give up on
each other
and circumstances.
We give up
on our mates
and family relationships.
We give up on
our children
and the challenges of parenting.
We give up on
the trials sent to train us
and the battles those
trials produce in the
private and social realm.
In our extreme despair,
we give up on life
and all hope of
Your sovereign control.
Oh, Lord, we give up on You.
Be strength in us
for the situations we
individually face
that we might stand together
a mighty army for God.
Take our eyes off
the destroyer
and fix them on the
Deliverer.
Teach us to press on
with courage
and walk by faith.

Hebrews 10:36 *For you have need of endurance, so that when you have done the will of God you may receive what is promised.*

Building

Lord,
This remodeling/building project
has turned into a
two and a half year nightmare.
More things have gone
wrong than right...
or have they gone
exactly according to Your purposes?
Walls torn out
expansion
progress
renovation
repair
of house and heart.
As tiny cracks in spirituality
widened and burst
to reveal the
desperate need
for dead and decayed
resolve
habit
stubborn determination
to be put off
and the new
Christ
put on.
Oh Father,
thank You for this old house
and for the new
improvements.

Ephesians 4:22-24 *To put off your old self, which belongs to your former manner of life and is corrupt through deceitful desires and to be renewed in the spirit of your minds, and to put on the new self, created after the likeness of God in true righteousness and holiness.*

Let Him Have His Way With You

Lord, I'm in a hard place.
"Child, you will grow there."
But it is such a hard place, Lord
and it has been so long!
"Child, it is working in you the gold of
trust and obedience."
Are You punishing me for failures
and inconsistencies?
"No, child of my heart.
I love you with an eternal love.
There is never
condemnation with Me,
only guidance and correction.."
And when I don't feel like
rejoicing?
"Rejoice anyway.
Rejoice in Me."
And when I don't feel like
giving thanks?
"Because you love Me,
regardless of circumstance,
offer Me the
sacrifices of praise and
thanksgiving.
I dwell in your praises.
In the practice of praise
You will find rest for the
weariness of your soul."
Oh, Lord,
truly I am Your servant.
You have loosed my bonds.
I will offer to You the
sacrifice of thanksgiving
and call upon the name of the Lord!

Psalm 116:16-17 *Oh Lord, I am your servant; I am your servant, the son of your maidservant. You have loosed my bonds. I will offer to you the sacrifice of thanksgiving and call upon the name of the Lord.*

Beauty Out of Ashes

It is a hard thing You are doing, Lord
this grinding down of my life.
Is it really necessary – this purging?
I read that You can take
the ashes of my life
and make the beauty of God...
beauty out of ashes
that is Your purpose in me.
There seems to be an endless supply
of selfish stuff in me for
purging, Lord.
But when the dross is
removed
the beauty of Your life is free
to shine forth through me
to the Glory of God!
Oh, Father,
bring beauty
out of the ashes
of my life
today.

Isaiah 61:3 ...*to grant to those who mourn in Zion—to give them a beautiful headdress instead of ashes, the oil of gladness instead of mourning, the garment of praise instead of a faint spirit; that they may be called oaks of righteousness, the planting of the Lord, that he may be glorified.*

One New Step

Father,
as I walk into
a new year
still in the darkness
of this present trial
teach me to look for
Your sparks of love
along the way.
Your glow of direction
and quiet, gentle leading
will not keep pace with my frenzy to
escape the waiting.
You tenderly call me
back to Your stride
to the glow of Your presence,
and You lead me
through the night
one new step at a time.

Psalm 33:18-22 *Behold, the eye of the Lord is on those who fear him, on those who hope in his steadfast love, that he may deliver their soul from death and keep them alive in famine. Our soul waits for the Lord; he is our help and our shield. For our heart is glad in him, because we trust in his holy name; Let your steadfast love, O Lord, be upon us, even as we hope in you.*

Restored

Oh Father,
if the many
broken
confused
bitter
angry
hurting people
pushed to the point
of divorce
would only
reach out across
the hurt
the anger
the wrongs done to each
and touch
heart to heart
soul to soul
need to need,
with the application
of Your heavenly adhesive
many a troubled marriage
could be restored.

Ecclesiastes 4:12 *Though one may be overpowered, two can defend themselves. A cord of three strands is not easily broken. (NIV)*

Children Search for Pieces

So many hurting people
try to throw away
their pain.
But in the tossing out of
sorrow
some joy is flung.
In the heaving of heaviness
some happiness is hurled.
Beautiful memories
are discarded with
broken dreams
the beauty all but forgotten.
And in the rubble of
broken lives
children search for
pieces of their own identity.
God help us.

Genesis 2:24 *Therefore a man shall leave his father and his mother and hold fast to his wife, and they shall become one flesh.*

Desperate Cries

In the next several entries, I hear the desperation in my voice as the words were penned, and remember fresh the feelings of defeat and despair I experienced as I read the Word, wrote, and prayed. Every morning seemed to bring a new battle, fresh with accusations of failure. I was convinced there was little my life had to offer anyone – particularly God. The accusations were as familiar as my mother's voice from childhood – *"You are stupid. You are just like your father. You will never amount to anything…Christine Marie, You Are HORRID!"* – and as fresh as the voices of church "friends" who pinned the failure of a spiritual leader on the shoulders of a woman manipulated by the evil of his perverted demands. The house was quiet enough in the early morning hours of those long nights-into-mornings for me to hear from God…His voice – literally – my salvation, my next breath.

I wonder if, as you read, you can identify with such desperation? The same God who heard my cries for rescue and release hears your voice today. He has not changed. He is the same yesterday, today and forever. Though my fight for life does not feel as desperate as it did then – in the early morning hours of every day – there are still times/seasons when the accusations rage.

The enemy is not very creative. He does not have a new plan. It is as old as Eden. He can only cast doubt. He can only tempt us to participate in the suggestion that God is trying to trick us – that He is holding out on us – that He is not enough. I pray that you will become so familiar with the Word of the Lover of your soul that you will remember His eternal love for you in those times when all you can hear are the hissings of Eden.

Terrors by Night

There is a suddenness
about the terror that
grips in fear
at night.
My breath shortens,
my heart quickens,
the icy bars of
confusion
close around my heart
and vibrate with
condemnation and contempt.

There is a subtleness
in the seduction that
taunts at noon.
It seeks to lure me
from the shelter of Your wings.
The enemy calls
with sweet breath
and careful word,
heating my desire
till I am blind with thirst
for things that will not
satisfy...
pierced through by the
arrows
of flattery.

Oh, Father,
In Your faithfulness
deliver me
from the terror at night
and the arrow at noon.
Hide me in the shelter of
Your wings
and rescue me

until this calamity
be over – past.

Psalm 91:4-5 *He will cover you with his pinions, and under his wings you will find refuge; his faithfulness is a shield and buckler. You will not fear the terror of the night, nor the arrow that flies by day…*

Through the Night

Father,
I am deep in despair.
Everywhere I look
there is darkness.
The waters rise
around my head
threatening to pull me under.
I am ill at rest
untrusting
thrashing about in spirit
cursing the things that
cloud my wants and ways
unwilling, or unable,
to see Your hand –
the weight of my burdens
smother and squelch
Your voice.
All seems to be
darkness and defeat.
My only thought is
Your justifiable right
to leave me
drowning in my own despair.
But You will never leave me.
Not even to my own
demise.
You come
ever faithfully
stroking my
tormented peace
and promise
Your faithfulness.
Like a loving mother
who sits by the
midnight bed

of a fevered child,
You sit with me
through the night.

Hebrews 13:5(b) ...*I will never leave you or forsake you.*

Cracks of Light

Father,
there is a
hopelessness
that clings to me.
It reaches deep into my soul
stifling my breath
robbing me of sleep
appetite
energy.
But when my knee is bent
and my head is bowed
and we commune,
there is a crack of light
through the hopelessness
and I can see
Your love.

Psalm 18:28 *For it is you who light my lamp; the Lord my God lightens my darkness.*

Looking In

Father,
this is a time of
self-help
of looking in
of taking inventory
of counting motives
mistakes
falling
following
living
loving, but it all wraps
in self.
I know looking in
is sometimes necessary
but help me not be
so enthralled with
looking in
that I forget to
look up.
I will never
unwrap the past
with understanding
until I first
accept it
as a gift of love
from You.

Psalm 43:5 *Why are you cast down, O my soul, and why are you in turmoil within me?*
Hope in God; for I shall again praise Him, my salvation and my God.

Perspective

Elisha's servant
saw the strength of the enemy
and trembled.
A wiser Elisha looked beyond
human scope
to heavenly horizon
full of angel warriors.

The sky blackened
at the crucifixion
and mourners wept
in silence
fleeing for their lives
from the host of unbelief
around them.
Fear drove them
into hiding
until the morning of the
resurrection
when their view
also lifted
above din of grave clothes
to glow of Risen Lord.

Today there is a
cloud of witnesses
surrounding us.
We plod along
head hung
eyes fixed on
dragging feet.
They faithfully cheer
"Look up!"
and whisper
Your promises in our
darkness.

Our rare glance becomes
a gaze – then a stare
eyes lifted from
din of day
to glow of our Hope in Christ
The Resurrection and the Life!

2 Kings 6:17 *Then Elisha prayed and said, "O Lord, please open his eyes that he may see." So the Lord opened the eyes of the young man, and he saw, and behold, the mountain was full of horses and chariots of fire all around Elisha.*

Releasing Control

Father,
My hands are small
they clutch at things they cannot hold
they seek to carry burdens
much too weighty for my frame.
They claw to control
circumstances that dangle
just out of reach.

Lord,
Your hands are big enough to hold
the world.
They carry all cares without
stagger or strain.
They cradle circumstances and all
the creatures involved.

Remind me in the midst of the
angry waves of this present trial
that it is Your voice that
calms the storm.
My own shrill cries are but a
flurry
of empty air.

1 Peter 5:7 *Cast all your cares on him because he cares for you. (NIV)*

The Interview

Oh Father,
on Monday I was on top
of the clouds
all seemed to go so well.
Thursday now lingers
each hour passes in
twice the usual time
the ticking of the clock
hurts my ears
and I am tuned
to every incoming call
waiting for my name
over loud speaker spoken
my emotions
rise and fall
with every blink
of the telltale "hold."

Let me not
wait
for man but for
God.
Have You not promised
to make me lie down
in green pastures?
To lead me beside
still waters?
To lead me in the
paths of righteousness
for Your name sake?
Whatever my desire, Lord,
I lay it down
content to take up my cross
and follow You –
all else is futile following and
disobedience.

Make clear the way for me,
for I desire to follow
You alone.

Psalm 43:3 *Send out your light and your truth; let them lead me.*

Sin Crouching

Sin is crouching at the door.
What a vivid picture painted.
Sin, belly to the ground
firearm in hand
aimed, geared for attack,
ready for battle.

Further warning –
And its desire is for you.
An assigned assassin
bent on my destruction.

The final call to alert –
But you MUST master it.
This does not suggest
passivity
but demands
affirmative action,
annihilation.

What will we then do?
Call upon the
Master of disaster
yield obediently to
Christ's command.
In His strength alone
we will overcome.

Genesis 4:6-7 *The Lord said to Cain, "Why are you angry and why has your face fallen? If you do well, will you not be accepted? And if you do not do well, sin is crouching at the door; its desire is for you, but you must rule over it."*

Noah

One faithful man
in the grip of a crooked
and perverse generation.
We might say the
influence
around us is too great
the pull too strong
the fight too hard
the army too weak,
too few.
Noah was one man
among many
wickedness on every side.
He was mocked for building
ship on dry land.
Chided for preaching flood
before rain existed.
Ridiculed for faith;
but Noah's eyes were fixed
on the God in whose loving eyes
he found grace.
What mockery do you face today?
What crippling chide or ridicule?
Do you look at accuser
or Advocate?
You, too, can find
grace
in the eyes of the Lord.

Genesis 6:8 *But Noah found grace is the eyes of the Lord. (NKJV)*

Moments

My heart is struck by these words today, Lord,
And there was evening
and there was morning
one day.
Father,
help me take this
one day
as just that –
one day.
Moment resting upon moment
and all in Your
capable hands.
Thank you that You
are Creator of
darkness
as well as light.
You created both
in one day.
Teach me to trust the
darkness
and light
of each new day
to Your care
knowing that You are the
Keeper
of all the moments of
my life.

Genesis 1:5 *God called the light day, and the darkness he called night. And there was evening and there was morning, one day. (NASB)*

Heritage

No matter my beginning
or the course
my life has taken;
my accomplishments
or defeats,
my joys,
or sorrows,
my desires fulfilled
or denied.
Still,
in Christ
my heritage is beautiful.
Truly His plan of
redemptive grace
has made my
wandering
through this life
a walk in pleasant places.
For with each step
He has drawn me
closer to His side.

Psalm 16:6 *The lines have fallen for me in pleasant places; indeed, I have a beautiful inheritance.*

My Soul Waits

In times of confidence
and doubt, God,
You are near.
It is such comfort to read
David's testimony:
My soul waits in
silence
for God only.
Yet, after reciting some
difficulties he had need to
remind himself with
quiet command,
My soul,
wait in silence for God only.
Oh, Lord,
thank you that Your promises
are a steadfast hope
in the midst of my
fluctuating emotions.

Psalm 62:1, 5 *Hear my cry, O God, listen to my prayer...For you, O God, have heard my vows; you have given me the heritage of those who fear your name.*

The Argument

We volley
contention and blame
he and I,
never looking
eye to eye
never reaching out
for one another.
There is no way
to climb out of this
pit of despair
except through You.
Lord,
grant us the
willingness to
transfer control
to You.

Ephesians 4:31-32 *Let all bitterness and wrath and anger and clamor and slander be put away from you, along with all malice. Be kind to one another, tenderhearted, forgiving one another, as God in Christ forgave you.*

The Transfer

Sometime during the day
it all shifted
from my perspective
to Yours.
My breath seems deeper
and more refreshing
not rapid and hot;
and there is a sigh of peace
deep within my heart.
The problems are no longer
mine alone;
they have been relieved
from my shoulders
and transferred to
Yours.
Oh, Father,
forgive me for waiting
so long
to let go.

Romans 12: 1-2 *I appeal to you therefore, brothers, by the mercies of God, to present your bodies as a living sacrifice, holy and acceptable to God, which is your spiritual worship. Do not be conformed to this world, but be transformed by the renewal of your mind, that by testing you may discern what is the will of God, what is good and acceptable and perfect.*

Bitter Sweet

Thank you
for showing me
again today
that when I come to Your table
hungry
I am always fed
abundantly –
Every bitter thing is sweet –
But when I come
to Your table
without an appetite
I don't even recognize
dessert!
And I leave Your
well-prepared
banquet table
so utterly empty and unsatisfied.

Proverbs 27:7 *One who is full loathes honey, but to one who is hungry everything bitter is sweet.*

Promises

Oh Father,
in the midst of the
day to day
problems
don't let me
forget
Your promises

Psalm 119:54 *Your statues have been my songs in the house of my sojourning.*

Misunderstanding

Two hurting people
One caring God
in three persons.
More than enough
love
for both.
Enough to share
enough to give away
enough to lavish
on the broken
and naked
and wretched
in the blindness of our
own way.
Enough to
cover
your sin
and mine
until we stand before Him
blameless
cleansed
from the stain of this
present misunderstanding.

Proverbs 10:12 *Hatred stirs up strife, but love covers all offenses.*

The Jailer

Imagine how the Jailer felt
when the quake at midnight
loosed the prisoners
he was told to guard
with his life.
All hope drained from him
terror set in;
certain there was
nothing left to do,
he drew his sword
to take his own life.
Have you been there?
I have.
In the midnight
of a trial or tragedy
all hope gone
every human resource
drained –
terror creeps in and settles.
Oh, friend,
don't end there…
for, like the Jailer,
when we come to the end
of ourselves
we are not at the end at all.
We are standing on the
brink
of a glorious new beginning.
The Jailer stepped
into the Light
that dark, terror-filled midnight.
How about you?

Acts 16:29-30 *And the jailer called for lights and rushed in, and trembling with fear he fell down before Paul and Silas. Then he brought them out and said, 'Sirs, what must I do to be saved?'*

Love Affair

Father,
I do not understand the
love affair
between my man and his work.
He seems consumed by it
obsessed.
He stays longer and longer
to accomplish less and less.
I weep for him when I see the
pit
others dig for him to walk in.
He is more worthy than all of them.
He is a man of great intelligence.
His hands are strong.
His ability is looked upon with honor
by those who care to see his heart.
But an enemy of overwhelming magnitude
has risen against him – against us.
It whispers words of
unfaithfulness to me
and neglect to his children.
This enemy steals his sleep
and his appetite.
The cruel destroyer will stop at
nothing
even confounding my prayers
when I cry out to You
for his release.
I have become weary and full of doubt,
like a dying woman clawing for life.
I no more know what to say
than what to do.
And when I do open my mouth
in an attempt to
comfort
I criticize.

When I would hold him in arms of
consolation and love
I abandon our bed in fear.
Releasing my life-draining grip
seems death to him
to me
to us.
But underneath are the
everlasting arms
and in the release
and in the fall
we will land in the very
center of Your grace.
You will then be free to
fight for us
the battle we are powerless to engage.
I need a King today, Lord.
Rule in power over this
strong enemy
and rescue us from
destruction.

Psalm 29:10-11 *The Lord sits enthroned over the flood; the Lord sits enthroned as king forever. May the Lord give strength to his people! May the Lord bless his people with peace!*

Spiritual Famine

Lord,
there is a famine in our land.
We starve for You
while we hold Your word
sing Your songs
and listen to sermons.
We are hungry
without cause
save our own reluctance to
Taste and see that the Lord is good.
Father,
You have promised
to keep us
alive in famine.
Open our eyes
to Your great provisions
before they are snatched
from us and we lie in the
sorrow
of our own neglect.

Psalm 33:18-19 *Behold, the eye of the Lord is on those who fear him, on those who hope in his steadfast love, that he may deliver their soul from death and keep them alive in famine.*

Winter

Father,
I am learning to
respect
appreciate
the barrenness of winter.
Trees stripped
revealing harsh lines
storm bents
twisted formations
frail branches.
There is an
intimacy
in their exposure.
In the winter we see
the REAL tree.
So are my times
of barrenness
before You, Lord.
When I admit my
harsh lines
storm bents
twisted formations
and frail branches,
You look on me
with a Creator's love
and assure me of
Your favor.
Because of Winter
the new birth and
blossom of Spring
will come to show Your glory.
You promised.

Isaiah 51:3 *For the Lord comforts Zion; he comforts all her waste places and makes her wilderness like Eden, her desert like the garden of the Lord; joy and gladness will be found in her, thanksgiving and the voice of song.*

Psalms Of My Heart

Psalms of Reorientation – Redemption

Redemption, n. | re•demp•tion| \ ri'dempSHən \

you might as well try to hear without ears or breathe without lungs, as to try

to live a Christian life without the Spirit of God in your heart. (D.L. Moody)

Introduction to Psalms of Reorientation – Redemption

"She would come rolling in a wave over you and leave you there on your behind choking on the thing you had intended to say. And she could keep coming with her flood and stand laughing at you struggling in the waves of your forgetting."
- K. Gibbons

"Mark my words, Mr. Rezendes, if it takes a village to raise a child, it takes a village to abuse one" (Spotlight, 2015).

I wanted June Cleaver to be my mother. She was the kind of mother who would see her little girl, wasn't she? I know she had boys – Beaver and Wally – but wouldn't she be equally concerned with a little girl? Yes, June Cleaver – or Donna Reed from *Father Knows Best*. My mother did not see me, hear me, or—in honest reality—love me. When she called me, answered me, or instructed me, it seemed to be with great effort and disdain, especially evident when she recited the HORRID nursery rhyme to me. Something about me was tainted or broken but I couldn't figure out what. I could clearly see that she loved my four siblings—two sisters 5 and 7 years older, and two brothers 4 and 8 years younger. I was smack dab in the middle, and there was definitely something wrong with me.

Take, for example, my twelfth birthday. The ear infection in my right ear had me down for several days and quickly graduated to a painful mastoid infection. To complicate matters, a staph infection had developed behind the affected ear in the crevice where ear and skull meet. The right side of my face was swollen twice the size of the left, and the ear so distended that it stuck straight out as if someone was pulling on it. Hot and bright red in color, it oozed a sticky yellow drain from the staph that stuck to my hair with a pungent aroma I could not wash away. I was in so much pain I could not bear to swallow much of anything. My mother scolded me considerably for not being able to swallow pills—even before the infection and the pain. To her credit, she tried many things—crushing them and mixing pill powder in peanut butter or applesauce to ease the medicine down. But on this particular morning it seemed she was on a mission to make me swallow the pill and in a hurry to get out the door to work. I would be left home alone until my oldest sister came to pick me up and take me to the doctor's office.

I could tell by the set of her jaw and the resolve in my mother's eyes that this would be the day I *would learn* to swallow a pill. "The doctor may put you in the hospital today and then you will have to swallow a *lot* of pills. You *will* learn how today before I go to work." The angry tremor in her voice frightened me. She stomped out of the room, where I was bedded, and returned with a tall glass full of water in one hand and a pill in the other. Her face was stone stern. "Remember the little girl with a pretty little curl? You do not want to be horrid today Chrissy…you *will* take this pill." I was thankful for the warning.

I opened my mouth wide so she could set the pill on the back of my tongue. She would not let me hold the glass but clenched my lower jaw tight in her angry hand, glass to my lips and began to tip the water in. Mouth puckered, throat tightened, and pain shot through my right ear as first swallow wrestled with a gag. The glass tipped higher – tried to wrangle my jaw from iron hand but her hold was solid. Couldn't breathe – still she tipped the glass higher – suffocating – drowning – tried again to squirm away – begged with eyes full of terror and tears – water leaking out the sides of my mouth –higher and higher she tipped until every drop of water was gone. At last, she yanked her hand away. I gasped for air for several minutes before I recovered breath. My pajamas were wet all the way down the front. When I looked up at her standing over me, her arms were folded across her chest and the smile on her face was a mixture of glee and triumph. "Swallowed it didn't you? Happy Birthday!" She turned triumphantly on one high heel and dashed out the door to work.

I was hospitalized that day. I remember the smell of clean, white hospital sheets, the comfort of the bed as it rested beneath me, and feeling safe as I closed my eyes and slept soundly. I didn't want to leave that hospital. And I remember getting a baby doll for my birthday–the exact one I wanted. In my child's mind, it is the only gift I remember receiving.

I was hospitalized for several days. Maybe the doctor felt sorry for me so he kept me as long as he could. I remember him being in my room the afternoon I was admitted. He witnessed my panic when I heard my mother's spiked heels ricochet off the hospital corridor walls. I broke into a cold sweat. I think I might have fainted. I remember him stroking my hand just before she walked in, telling me it would be okay. There was no mistaking her forceful, angry gait, and it was an awful inconvenience to have to stop by the hospital on her way home from work. She said so as she handed me my gift.

When I was discharged from the hospital, my mother remarked that people were staring at me being wheeled out of the hospital because I looked like a new mother with that baby doll cradled in my arms, and I was so young. I soaked in those comments then in my innocence–to be thought of as a new mother at twelve–but I wonder now why her remarks to me were often about looking pregnant, accusing me of being pregnant, or looking like a new mother…remarks that were consistently filled with sarcasm and contempt. No, my mother was not even close to embodying June Cleaver or Donna Reed.

As a child who was a disappointment in many ways–but initially because I was born a girl–and as a child who suffered multiple forms of abuse, the bulk of my earliest memories are associated with suffering. In the midst of those difficult, painful, destructive, and frightening years, however, there were also many moments of comfort and joy.

It was during my early childhood years of suffering that I developed a keen sense of God's presence. All of my senses–sight, smell, taste, touch, and hearing–were heightened with anticipation of connection with the God of my Gram–my great grandmother. She lived in the duplex directly above ours with my Uncle Ed and Aunt Lola. She was bedridden for as long as I knew her. I'm not sure what her illness was, but I can remember that she let me climb up on her big iron bed housed in the room just off the living room. There were windows all around that long, skinny room, which–in my memory–was just big enough for her double bed, a nightstand, a rocking chair, and a chest of drawers. The floors were scuffed wood, and there was a small, flat, oval matted bathroom rug beside the bed. It took some doing to hoist my small 4-year-old frame onto that big bed but, when I did, Gram would tell me stories about Jesus, talk about her love for Him, and recite Bible verses to me while I brushed her long, beautiful, silver hair. These are some of my most precious childhood memories. She spoke very softly and not often, but if she heard Uncle Ed talking to me or asking me to come into his study, she would call to me, "Chrissy…Chrissy dear, come in here for a moment, please." I don't know if she knew about or sensed the sexual abuse I experienced at his hands, nonetheless, she never failed to call me away from him. In the end, he abused me during naptime, which was in a room in another part of the house where Gram could not hear.

I remember the day Gram died. The family stood around her bed–I'm not sure what we were doing–but I know she died peacefully and was as beautifully radiant in death as she was in life.

It would be sixteen long and difficult years before I embraced Gram's God as my own, but I knew what the presence of God was even as a neglected, abandoned, and abused little girl because of my Gram's love for both Jesus and me. I don't know if this is the truth, but I believe it was Gram who taught me to memorize Hebrews 13:5, *"I will never leave thee" (KJV)*. It was a truth I firmly believed and clung to throughout my childhood and adolescence, teaching it to my children when they were very young.

After becoming a Christian at age twenty, my life changed drastically—from the broken, lost little child I was to a vivacious young woman. By age twenty-one, my world included a husband and baby, and two more followed shortly thereafter. I loved my family, loved God, and longed to know Jesus more and more. I read my first Bible so much the binding broke loose from its pages—I could not get enough of the Word. I wanted to know Jesus with everything that was in me. At the same time, I struggled to feel worthy of His love, or even worthy of life itself. My suffering continued in the form of doubts and fears about losing God's presence and love in my life. I became a very legalistic, performance-based believer. I was kept alive in childhood by keeping the rules—even though the rules my mother dictated were constantly changing. As much as I knew I loved God, I could not understand that the power with which He saved me was the same power that would keep me.

Yes, evil claimed me during my very early years. I was daily reminded that I was stupid and would never amount to anything...the label HORRID was regularly reinforced and I fully embraced it. This was my agreement with evil. I saw myself as HORRID without hope of ever being different. And when, as a Christian young woman, I fell prey to a predator the label felt "seared into my flesh."

For many years after that devastating abuse, my husband and I struggled, emotionally separated yet under the same roof, and under the same weight of horrendous trauma—long past and not so distant. And I blamed myself for it all. My husband and I were convinced that I was at fault, which set up a tension in our home that, at times, took us to the very brink of despair. Our home was a cesspool of contempt and shame, and I deeply grieve the years our children had to navigate in the caustic atmosphere we created.

In those dark and desperate years, God continued to draw us each into His strong embrace. He never failed to open a window of hope when despair closed over me with a disabling darkness. Many biblical figures have known this "dark night of the soul," and have clung to God as He walked with them through the long moments, hours, days, months, and sometimes years of the process of reorientation. Job is probably the most well-known of these biblical figures.

There is a deep joy in the reality of orientation; a rending despair in the traverse of lament; yet a steady and sanctioned goodness in the hope that leads to reorientation and the will to love again.

God worked His will in us separately through many of those years of lament, then gave us opportunity to walk through a darkness of shared lament, which brought us to a place of new beginning. In the cold, January winter of 2008, my husband was diagnosed with Chronic Obstructive Pulmonary Disease (COPD) along with two additional incurable lung conditions – mycobacterium avium complex (MAC) and bronchiectasis. The devastation of this addition to our already strained relationship periodically engulfed and paralyzed me. I felt abandoned by God and left alone to face a future without a husband. We had been emotionally separated for many years, but the threat of being without my husband stopped me in my tracks, and called me to consider who this man was and what we now had created by clinging to our hope that God would bring our marriage out of darkness and into the light again.

On one particularly dark afternoon when my faith was barely a flicker, a familiar feeling of foreboding and fear engulfed me and threatened to drag me under. My husband's recent diagnosis birthed deep wells of fear, which seemed to pile up on top of the significant weight of the trials I already carried. I staggered under the strain of it all. Taken individually, the weight would not have threatened me – maybe. But on this day, I was feeling overwhelmed as I stepped into my bedroom hideaway to be alone with God. It was a quiet place and a safe place to talk out loud to God. I rehearsed my fears and feelings of foreboding to Him and sensed His calming presence over me. As I closed my eyes, my thoughts went to a rock ledge near Malibu on the Pacific Coast where my sister and I sat for hours, talked, laughed, and marveled at God's creation. We stayed until the tide came in under a blanket of purple and gold and the sun slipped silently – gloriously – into the sea.

In a moment, I was sitting again on the rock ledge and begging Jesus to come and join me there. As I meditated on His comfort, I saw Him walk toward me on the waves of the sea that were gently lapping at the shore. I extended my hand, and He pulled me up from my squatted position on the rock. As I fell into Jesus' embrace, He began to dance me across the top of the waves. It was a glorious glide with frequent sprays of wind and wave on my face. It was a peaceful place void of foreboding and fear.

Suddenly, the winds increased and the waves complied with dips and peaks that white-capped at our feet. I could feel fear threaten my peace and begin a storm of doubt in my soul. Jesus tightened His embrace and whispered, "It's just a wave, Christine. The waves may white cap at our feet; they may lurch and roll, peak and foam, but I will be with you; I will hold you, and we will dance across the storm. Rest in Me, Christine. It's just a wave."

After a long moment, I opened my eyes; I was still sitting in the safety of my room; my face wet with tears – tears of refreshing – and my heart filled with the stilled, peaceful silence only Christ can bring. "What manner of man is this, that even the wind and the sea obey Him?" (see Matthew 8:27 and Mark 4:41). As I walked out into the frenzy of my earthy world, I softly whispered the reminder, "It's just a wave," my arms formed a self-embrace; I looked heavenward and I smiled.

This experience/encounter of faith was a place of new beginning for me. It is a scene to which I have often returned as the waves have again begun to lurch and roll, peak and foam. I remember He is with me; He will hold me, and He will dance me across the storm. My part is to rest in Him, to trust Him, and to remember, "…even the wind and the sea obey Him. It's just a wave."

In this last section of *Psalms,* you will continue to see my struggle with darkness tucked into many of the writings, but you will also see the light of redemption dawning brighter and brighter on my soul, our lives, and our home.

Encouragement

Father,
I have complete confidence
that You can
overcome
any difficult situation
circumstance
or experience.
Even in the darkness of the
crucifixion,
You knew
there would be
a resurrection.

1 Corinthians 15:54 ...*death is swallowed up in victory.* *(NAS)*

Our Home

Father,
forgive me for my
covetous feelings
for our old house
today.
Tonight,
safe and secure
in the arms of my
loving husband
I imagined You
smiling down
on Your
victorious work
of restoration
in our marriage
and at that moment
I knew again
that You have
already granted me
the desires of my heart.
Our love
is what makes
this house
our home.
Thank you, Lord.

2 Corinthians 13:11 *Finally, brothers, rejoice. Aim for restoration, comfort one another, agree with one another, live in peace; and the God of love and peace will be with you.*

Victorious

Father,
I am so thankful
that You are
in complete control.
Though our lives
are under attack
on every side,
though the enemy
appears to gain
victory after victory,
though all honor
truth and righteousness
seems stifled
even snuffed out at times,
in You we truly are not permanently
distressed
in despair
forsaken
or destroyed.
In You
we are always
victorious.

2 Corinthians 4:8-9 *We are afflicted in every way, but not crushed; perplexed, but not driven to despair; persecuted, but not forsaken; struck down, but not destroyed.*

Entering Your Presence

Father,
help me learn to
build on heavenly principles
not earthly motives.
I want to
enter Your presence
with a confident glow
and a sweet smell;
not with traces of soot
and the stench of smoke.

1 Corinthians 3:14-15 *If the work that anyone has built on the foundation survives, he will receive a reward. If anyone's work is burned up, he will suffer loss, though he himself will be saved, but only as through fire.*

Fill All of Me

Forgive me for being unloving –
and teach me to love.

Forgive my selfishness –
and teach me to serve.

Forgive my periodic silence –
and teach me to tell.

Forgive my self-reliance –
and teach me to trust.

Forgive my slothful attitudes –
and teach me to work.

Forgive my rebellion –
and teach me to submit.

Forgive my empty boastings –
and teach me humility.

Forgive my foolish pride –
and teach me to be teachable.

Empty me completely of self
and fill all of me with You.

Psalm 37:3 *Trust in the Lord and do good; dwell in the land and befriend faithfulness.*

Redeemed

Father,
help me let go of
greed
covetousness
pride
jealously
rebellion
stubbornness
lust
anger
doubt
deceit –
for they are
the fetters
that bind me to this world.
Let me rise above
the evils of this life
and experience to the fullest
the joy of being
REDEEMED!

Isaiah 44:22 *I have blotted out your transgressions like a cloud and your sins like mist; return to me, for I have redeemed you.*

Faithful & Obedient

Father,
when Samuel came
to anoint him,
David was not in a place
of prominence.
He was not even
invited
to the banquet.
He was out in the field
tending sheep,
faithfully doing
what You called him to do.
Teach me to
stay in the field
to tend
to serve
diligently performing
those things You have
given me to do
so that when You come
I will be found
faithful and obedient.

Matthew 25:23 *His master said to him, 'Well done, good and faithful servant. You have been faithful over a little; I will set you over much. Enter into the joy of your master.'*

The Fountain

Sometimes I struggle
with rhymes and rhythm.
I try to say too much
or sound too profound.
Help me grasp the
simple truth
You are teaching me today;
when the words come from
You
and not from me
they flow like the fountain
that flows within me.

John 4:14 ...*but whoever drinks of the water that I will give him will never be thirsty again. The water that I will give him will become in him a spring of water welling up to eternal life.*

Your Eternal Love

Father,
I do not ever want
to become complacent
satisfied
with a meager existence
in You.
Teach me to seek to know
the very breadth
and height
and width
and depth
of Your Eternal Love.

Romans 8:38-39 *For I am sure that neither death nor life, nor angels nor rulers, nor things present nor things to come, nor powers, nor height nor depth, nor anything else in all creation, will be able to separate us from the love of God in Christ Jesus our Lord.*

The Tongue

Lord,
I am so often
quick to speak;
words tumble out
ripping
tearing
leaving unintentional wounds.
A small thought
once spoken
consumes the room
and will not fit again
into the place of its birth.
It is gone forever
carrying out its
wild appointment.

Teach me to speak
with wisdom.
Let me not open my mouth
without first giving You
quick inventory of the
words that are hidden
in my heart.

Psalm 19:14 *Let the words of my mouth and the meditation of my heart be acceptable in your sight, O Lord, my rock and my redeemer.*

Busy Day

Father,
help me take time out of
this busy day
to enjoy
this busy day;
to show love
to my little ones
and hear their requests,
their opinions,
with interest;
to respond to their needs
and the needs of my husband
with joy.
Help my life
even in late afternoon
reflect the fact
that I have
enjoyed
the light of Your presence
this morning.

Matthew 5:16 *In the same way, let your light shine before others, so that they may see your good works and give glory to your Father who is in heaven.*

Father, Forgive Me

Father,
forgive my insensitivity
my boastfulness
my pride
my rebellion.
I always learn late
that when I think
everyone else's life
should be improved
or changed
or more conformed to You,
I am usually the one
standing the farthest
away.

Matthew 7:1-3 *Judge not, that you be not judged. For with the measure you use it will be measured to you. Why do you see the speck that is in your brother's eye, but do not notice the log that is in your own eye?*

Conforming

Oh Father,
trying to conform
to fit in
to the friendships
of the world
I have become
out of joint with You.
I bring You the
pieces
and ask You
to fit me together again
with the adhesives of
truth and righteousness.

Peter 1:14 *As obedient children, do not be conformed to the passions of your former ignorance…*

Fools

In Proverbs
Your words says
that fools
despise wisdom,
sport to do mischief,
are right in their own eyes,
are instantly angry
and rage with confidence,
despise your instruction,
speak foolishness,
meddle,
and rebel.
Oh Father,
please forgive me
for acting like a
fool.

Ephesians 5:15 *Look carefully then how you walk, not as unwise but as wise.*

Frail

Father,
we speak of
days yet to come
months
even years
as if we are somehow
timeless,
indestructible.
Oh that we would
realize
how frail
we really are.

Psalm 39:4 *Oh Lord, make me know my end and what is the measure of my days; let me know how fleeting I am!*

Whisperings

Father,
teach me to
incline my ear to
Your words of knowledge
and take away
my desire
to hear and follow
the wandering whisperings
of the enemy.

Proverbs 19:27 *Cease to hear instruction, my son, and you will stray from the words of knowledge.*

Marching

Oh Father,
it grieves me
that I so easily
go astray.
After reading and studying
and hearing taught
The battle is not yours –
but God's –
I marched stalwartly
out on my own
yesterday,
armor askew
temper flaring;
and in that first step
met defeat.
Do You think I will
ever learn
to march in perfect cadence
to Your will?
I wonder, Lord.

1 John 1:7 *But if we walk in the light, as he is in the light, we have fellowship with one another, and the blood of Jesus his Son cleanses us from all sin.*

Turn in Truth

Oh Father,
that my heart would
turn to You
in truth;
that every motive would find
its origin in You,
and each accomplishment
would not be the least bit
inclined to clap
for its cooperation
with Your Spirit –
that every hand
outstretched
would have Your
genuine touch
and each smile
would be lit with the glow
of a heart aflame with Your love.
That my life
would be flung open wide
not with a careless
crowd-pleasing gesture,
but in subtle surrender to
My Sovereign King.
Oh, that my heart
would turn to You
in truth.

John 3:21 *But whoever does what is true comes to the light, so that it may be clearly seen that his works have been carried out in God.*

The Ministry of Reconciliation

Father,
help me realize
I have not been sent
to straighten out
anyone.
This sterile
judgmental approach
causes many to
shun You.
Rather, I have been given
the ministry of
reconciliation,
which is to offer
new life
to dead men and women.
You are the One Who
arouses their attention
and invites their response.
I simply hold the treasure
You extend
for them to examine.
Oh Father,
may I consecrate my life
to You
that I might be a
rightful representative.

2 Corinthians 4:7 *But we have this treasure in jars of clay, to show that the surpassing power belongs to God and not to us.*

Mary

Lord,
The Mary in me
wants to linger at Your feet
and let every precious word
soak deep into my spirit,
but the Martha in me
is too busy
making provision for the flesh.
Incorporate Your
beautiful balance
in me
so that I might
experience
the fullness of Your joy
while fulfilling
my responsibilities.

Luke 10:40-42 *But Martha was distracted with much serving. And she went up to him (Jesus) and said, 'Lord, do you not care that my sister has left me to serve alone? Tell her to help me.' But the Lord answered her, 'Martha, Martha, you are anxious and troubled about many things, but one thing is necessary. Mary has chosen the good portion, which will not be taken away from her.'*

Your Bounty

Father,
today I see it.
No wonder I have been
walking in defeat.
I have not been
inclining my ear
applying my heart
crying after knowledge
lifting up my voice for understanding
seeking and searching
for truths
revealed in Your word.
I have been content
with a small appetite
for the things of God,
which has left me not only
hungry
but starving.
Thank You, Father,
for the Holy Spirit,
who shows me
my bony skeletons of
wisdom and understanding.
The table is set,
and I am ready
to feast on
the bounty You have prepared.

Proverbs 2:2-5 …*making your ear attentive to wisdom and inclining your heart to understanding; yes, if you call out for insight and raise your voice for understanding, if you seek it like silver and search for it as hidden treasures, then you will understand the fear of the Lord and find the knowledge of God.*

Narrow Walls

The disciples
could not comprehend
the Resurrection
before it occurred.
You taught them in
so many ways
that You would
rise again.
They kept looking for
Your overthrow
of Roman rule,
imagined You as
earthly king.
What better plan could there be?
The human mind could not
conceive
an empty tomb
as they wept over the body
of their crucified conqueror.
The men all but
vanished into hiding,
locking away the promise
of resurrection
even from their memory.
It was the soldiers who
made the grave secure,
fearing Your escape
showing more faith
in Your proclamation
that You would rise again
than Your own disciples.
We have not changed much
have we, Lord?
You give so freely
of Your promises
a book full;

yet we choose the
narrow walls
of our own understanding.

Proverbs 3:5-6 *Trust in the Lord with all your heart, and do not lean on your own understanding. In all your ways acknowledge him, and he will make straight your paths.*

Driven

Lord,
I am a child
driven
to do great things for You.
House organized
kids organized
work organized
church organized
husband organized
(manageable).
Imperfect goals of
perfection.
STOP!
Lord,
teach me to be
led
not driven.
I am tired of screaming
demands at deaf ears
insisting my way best.
We both know
self has taken place of
Spirit.
Forgive me.
I give You back the
reigns of control
and suddenly
all aspects of life and love
align aright.

Psalm 23:2 *He makes me lie down in green pastures. He leads me beside still waters.*

Words

Father,
I am a writer of
words.
A group of
subjects
verbs
adjectives
phrases
strung together
to express
feelings
ideas
impressions
beliefs.
Help the foundation
of my poetry and prose
be totally based
on the power of Your word,
not on my own
interpretation.

Hebrews 4:12 *For the word of God is living and active, sharper than any two-edged sword, piercing to the division of soul and of spirit, of joints and of marrow, and discerning the thoughts and intentions of the heart.*

Preservatives

Like a
jar of jelly
I am being preserved
by the ingredients
of integrity and
uprightness.
Father,
I ask You to
keep me fresh
lest the taste of
my witness
be spoiled.

Psalm 25:21 *May integrity and uprightness preserve me, for I wait for you.*

Don't Let Me Sleep

When the disciples
went to the garden with Jesus
they were told to
watch and pray,
but, instead,
they fell asleep.
Just now
the world is so in need
of You.
It is time to
watch and pray,
go and tell.
Father,
don't let me
go to sleep.

Matthew 9:37-38 *Then he said to his disciples, 'The harvest is plentiful, but the laborers are few; therefore pray earnestly to the Lord of the harvest to send out laborers into his harvest.'*

Focus

There is no day longer
than the day we spend
worrying about ourselves.

There is no day shorter
than the day we spend
meeting the needs of others.

Father, please keep my priorities in focus.

2 Corinthians 13:11 *Finally, brothers, rejoice. Aim for restoration, comfort one another, agree with one another, live in peace; and the God of love and peace will be with you.*

Time to Clean the Gutters

Lord,
He put it off too long, and now the leaves are so thick in the gutters above the boys' windows that the rain is gushing over the gutter, down the window and leaking into the house. There is water all over the wall, and the carpet is soaked.

He has been so busy working he has not had time to clean them. Now, in the middle of a downpour of rain, he is getting drenched raking leaves out of the gutter so the water can run down the drain pipe and onto the ground.

Your voice speaks, my heart cries. I hear You, Lord.

How much like my own life it is. I allow little "leaves" of sin to stay in the channel of my life. One by one they collect and block Your word, Your will; until, in the midst of a downpour of trial, trouble, sickness, rebuke, I call out at last for cleansing.

Father, clean out the collection of sin in me so that the Holy Spirit can flow freely through me. And Father, help me keep up the maintenance on my channel through daily cleansing.

The Pharisee

Lord,
tear from me the Pharisee in me
who makes such grand display
of prayer requests and lists
but forgets to pray.

Lord,
tear from me the Pharisee in me
who labors to have "quiet time"
by early morning light
but screams at child and husband
that same night.

Lord,
tear from me the Pharisee in me
who lectures long of love
of giving and forgiving
of sacrifice and thankful heart
yet sulks and scorns with angry fists
at even slight injustices.

Lord,
tear from me the Pharisee in me
who claims a faithful partnership
a tried and true discipleship
among the believing few,
but feigns the opportunity
in masses of humanity
to speak of one's eternity
apart from You.

Lord,
tear from me the Pharisee in me
the white-washed sepulcher and cup
full of dead men's bones and filth within –
the old man tries so hard to win!

Deep cleanse me, Lord
fill me anew
that I might show my world
You.

Matthew 23:25-28 *Woe to you, scribes and Pharisees, hypocrites! For you clean the outside of the cup and the plate, but inside they are full of greed and self-indulgence. You blind Pharisee! First clean the inside of the cup and the plate, that the outside also may be clean.*

Little Flowers

So often my little ones
will stop their busy play outside
to bring me a
just-picked flower.
With little eyes lit up,
they march toward me,
wearing an unquenchable grin
their gift held proudly
in their little extended hand.
"This is for you, mommy!
Isn't it pretty?"
Oh, Lord,
I wonder how long it's been
since I've taken time from my
daily activities
to bring You a little flower;
to thank You for Your love for me;
to do something for another in Your name
without fanfare
hesitation
or grumbling;
to share Your love with
a broken heart
or an unborn spirit;
to give unselfishly
to rejoice with another
without envy?
How long, Father?
Teach me to pick the
little flowers along the way
for You,
not because I have to
but just to show my love for You.

1 John 3:18 *Little children, let us not love in word or talk but in deed and in truth.*

Praise Him

Father,
thank you
for treading down my enemies,
for lifting my head
above the waves of confusion and death;
for setting my feet
upon the Solid Rock,
for hiding me with Christ in You;
for guiding my way,
for our quiet talks,
for Your tender chastisement
and loving hug of forgiveness;
for Your complete loss of memory
over my confessed sin;
for Your promises in life
and privileges in death;
for showing me every day
the best is always yet to come
in You.

Psalm 34:1-3 *I will bless the Lord at all times; his praise shall continually be in my mouth. My soul makes its boast in the Lord; let the humble hear and be glad. Oh, magnify the Lord with me, and let us exalt his name together!*

Your Resting Place

Father,
forgive me for struggling
to rest in the strength of my own
resources.
You are not a stone statue
with deaf ears
and immobile hands.
You are
the One True and Living God.
my Fortress,
my Refuge,
the Lifter up of my head,
my Rock,
the God in whom I can trust,
my Buckler,
my Hiding Place,
the Strength of my life.
You are the only One
to whom I can run and find
strength to help in the time of need,
peace and rest in the midst of the
storms of life.
Thank you, Father,
for the perfect provision
and safety
of Your resting place.

Psalm 46:1 *God is our refuge and strength, a very present help in trouble.*

Sweet Comfort

Wonderful moments of pleasure divine.
Oh, what a joy that I feel!

Knelt here beside You before Your great throne,
Your presence within me so real!

Thoughts that are hidden deep down in my heart,
Glory, oh Glory, You see!

Here in the midst of my turmoil and strife,
You bring sweet comfort to me!

Psalm 94:19 *When the cares of my heart are many, your consolations cheer my soul.*

Every Knee/Every Tongue

Unbelievers scoff and mock Your name, Lord,
blame You
curse You
spit on You
with wicked words
unknowing
that one day
every knee
every tongue
will bow to Your Holiness
and confess Your Majesty.
Oh Lord,
how much is eternally lost
in what unseeing hearts call
winning.

Philippians 2:10-11 ...*so that at the name of Jesus every knee should bow, in heaven and on earth and under the earth, and every tongue confess that Jesus Christ is Lord, to the glory of God the Father.*

Worthy Art Thou O Lord

Father,
I long to dance through the days
praising You
just for Who You are –
without a trace of trouble
invading my thoughts
without a moan of self-pity
without a complaint of circumstance –
just continual praise.
But I embrace the earthly
just the same for now.
It is the stuff that drives me
to my knees.
It is the reason for my
desperate reliance;
it is the heavenly x-ray
of my hopeless condition
one moment apart from You.
And so I praise You with this
weight of flesh about me
in imperfection with the
Spirit of God
to intercede.

But then…
face-to-face
around the throne
with throng of four-and-twenty elders
saying day and night.

Revelation 4:11 *Worthy art Thou, Our Lord and Our God to receive glory and honor and power, for You created all things, and by Your will they existed and were created.*

Everlasting Love

Father,
what a loving parent
You are.
You purchased eternal life
for me
through Your son, Jesus.
You gave this gift
freely.
Though I have often neglected
this precious gift,
You have forgiven.
Your love is so great for me
that when I wander,
You seek after me;
when I stumble,
You steady my step;
when I fall,
You reach down with tender hands
and draw me close
to Your side
to assure me of Your
restoration.
Your voice is always
tender and loving.
Your chastisement is swift.
Your judgments are sure.
Considering Your
everlasting love and faithfulness
I bow my heart
and ask You to help me be
a better child.

Jeremiah 31:3(b) *I have loved you with an everlasting love. (NAS)*

Triumphant

Father,
when I look at the
drudgery
defeat
disease
despair
of life
through the eyes of my flesh
I waver in faith –
I falter.
But when I view
life's disappointments
through the Light of Your promises,
and the Victory of the Cross,
in everything
I am triumphant!

2 Corinthians 2:14-15 *But thanks be to God, who in Christ always leads us in triumphal procession, and through us spreads the fragrance of the knowledge of him everywhere. For we are the aroma of Christ to God among those who are being saved and among those who are perishing.*

Fragments of Failure

Matthew 26:75 *And Peter remembered the saying of Jesus…and he went out and wept bitterly.*

Peter knew shame.
He also knew
Your healing touch of
restoration.
I am one such as Peter, Lord.
Allow my wounds of wandering
to become a secret source
of inner strength –
a well of delight
flowing from the mountain of my
Redeemer God.
Peter never wrote of his failure,
only of Your strength.
Make of the fragments of my failure
a feast of refreshment.
And in that silent surrender
of weakness
become my Strength.

John 6:12 … *Gather up the leftover fragments, that nothing may be lost.*

Forgiveness

Father,
I begged and begged for
Your forgiveness
over a failure of years gone by.
Still the dark clouds of guilt
hung over me
until they choked the joy
out of my rejoicing.
My soul was heavy,
my well seemed to dry up
completely.
I read my Bible daily
and sought You with tears.
At last in the quiet of a
morning hour
not particularly set aside
for asking,
I listened for Your whisper
and it came
with power and conviction.
A familiar line from Matthew,
Forgive us our debts
as we forgive
our debtors.
At once I saw the dam of
bitterness and resentment
that blocked the flow of
Your Spirit.
Oh, Love Divine,
all loves excelling!
Praise You, Father,
for the glorious gift
of forgiveness
it is the key to
freedom from

guilt, shame, and despair.
I will rest now in the
glory
of Your unfailing love.

Jude 24-25 *Now to him who is able to keep you from stumbling and to present you blameless before the presence of his glory with great joy, to the only God, our Savior, through Jesus Christ our Lord, be glory, majesty, dominion, and authority, before all time and now and forever. Amen.*

Alone?

When I walked through the
dark
black hour
of loneliness
sorrow
pain
confusion
loss
it seemed so senseless.
You seemed so far away.
I searched for You
sometimes only glimpsing
flashes of light
brief
fleeting.
I felt deserted – alone.
But You were there
always loving me
encouraging me to
hunger
to thirst
for You.
And when at last the
search
was ended and I stepped
full into Your Light
it was more glorious
than I had ever remembered!

Psalm 23:3 *He restores my soul…*

Burdens

There are times, Lord,
when the weight of the world
seems to rest on my shoulders
as a result of
disobedience
worry
or sorrow.
Your promise in Psalms to
remove my shoulder from the burden
brings great release.
I envision a strong hand
coming between myself and the
heavy load.
You also remind me that
obedience
trust
and faith
are the feathery fetters
of Your love
that enable me to
soar above the
pressing ponderosity
and rest
in the arms of
Your perfect peace.

Matthew 11:28-30 *Come to me, all who labor and are heavy laden, and I will give you rest. Take my yoke upon you, and learn from me, for I am gentle and lowly in heart, and you will find rest for your souls. For my yoke is easy, and my burden is light.*

Christ Formed in Me

Father,
I have been so slow to acknowledge
the worth of life's unpleasantries–
disappointments
disillusionments
discouragements
rejection.
Rather than releasing all
to Your capable care,
I have relived
over and over again
the pain, failure, and shame
of the past –
and the frustration
of the present.

Today, Father,
I can finally see
how You are sweetly,
patiently
showing me
that I must learn to die.
Die to my fretful childhood
to unfortunate circumstances
to irritations
and inconsistencies
in myself and others
to sadness
pain
depression and loss –
to all the everyday dealings
of life.
To look beyond the
immediate drudge
and see the

ultimate glow
of Christ formed in me.

Romans 8:18 *For I consider the sufferings of this present time are not worth comparing with the glory that is to be revealed to us.*

Open Hands

When I was a little girl
I used to cling
with fists full of clothing
to my mother's skirt
or my father's trousers.
When I grew older,
I still grasped for that
security
with the hidden hands
of emotional need.
When I became a wife
I tried to cling to my mate,
but he would not be held
in such a disabling embrace.
As the children came
I found I could only hold them
tightly for a while;
soon their need to be
independent
was hindered by my
clutches,
and they became
resentful and rebellious.
The more I clung
whether to moments of time
or memories
the more I seemed to lose my
grip on life…
until by Your grace
You showed me the freedom
of open hands.

Now I can
let go of the little girl
and be a woman.
I can let go of the man

and be a wife.
I can let go of the children
and be a mother,
not looking for my fulfillment
in them
but finding my fulfillment
in You –
secure in the
hollow of Your hand.
It is a mystery, Lord,
but in the release of
my demands
my expectations
my control
all that would not be held
often seek my company
and the comfort they can find
in the security of my
open hands.

Psalm 88:9 ...*I spread out my hands to you.*

His Grace in Me

In my open hand I held
a little bunch of seeds
unearthed when I discovered
childhood crops destroyed by weeds.

My Savior held His hand out
and bid me place them there
where they were open and exposed
to water, light, and air.

He swept me up in His embrace
And took me to a field
That fresh was tilled and ready
with a promise of full yield.

I sorrowed over buried seed
and doubted any good
could come from such a mangled mass
of dirt and rot and wood,

But through the cold and wind and rain
the tender buried pods
died to be born an altered life
a planting of the Lord.

Now as I sit beneath the shade
of all that's come to be
surrendered seeds of childhood loss
reveal His grace in me.

John 12:24 *Truly, truly, I say to you, unless a grain of wheat falls into the earth and dies, it remains alone, but if it dies, it bears much fruit.*

Husbands, Wives, Mothers and Fathers

Love

Guarded glances
holding hands
first kisses
dates
desire
proposal
engagement
tiresome planning
wedding bells
honeymoon
back to work
cooking school
morning sickness
bundle of joy
earaches
colic
first tooth
first words
first steps
childhood diseases
"Daddy's home"
walks in the park
the zoo
first grade
PTA
music lessons
promotion for Dad
football games
Mom's taxi service
first date
driving lessons
shattered nerves!
class ring
Term paper tomorrow?

Graduation!
Late night talks
some mountains
some valleys
some sorrows
more joys.
Life for us is still
unfolding
like a beautiful flower
fragrant
fragile
full of wonder.
Sharing life with you
has been one of God's
greatest gifts to me.
I love you, Honey,
Happy Valentine's Day!

Genesis 2:18 *Then the Lord God said, 'It is not good that man should be alone; I will make him a helper fit for him.'*

The Miracle of it All

I stood sideways today
checking my swollen form
for a glimpse of who I
used to be –
slender
carefree
a woman, a wife.
I suddenly cradled my arms
around my abdomen
trying to imagine
holding you
seeing you face to face
blessing of God
miracle of love
perfect image of
your father and I
one
in human form.
I have prayed for your
growth
your digits
your "secret parts."
I have thanked God
for your first kick
and giggled to see your father
astonished
as you rolled from one
side of me
to the other.
I have cried over my
inadequacies
and thrilled at the prospect
of your life in my arms.
Soon, little one,
you will arrive and my life
will be changed forever.

I will no longer be only
a daughter, a woman,
a sister, a wife.
I will enter the awesome world
of motherhood.
I may
hold you wrong
scold you long,
not listen when you call –
cry
complain
fail
spoil
but underneath us both
will be the
love of God –
deep
wide
all consuming
and capable
of first babies
new mothers
and the miracle of it all.

Psalm 139:17 *How precious are your thoughts toward me, O God! How vast is the sum of them!*

Motherhood

A mysterious feeling
came over me
when I first held you.
A mixture of total inadequacy
yet confidence
in helping you become
all you would one day
dream to be.
I was so undiscerning of the
treasures that lay in store
for me.
From the first snuggle of your
tiny face against my face
your fuzzy little head
tucked under my chin
your sweet sleeping breath
and the little grunts of
contentment you cooed –
to the pure delight
of my lips on the bottoms
of your warm little feet –
you were wanted.
I love the way you
wake up the morning
your happiness flooding into
every room.
I love your joyful laughter
and the way your mouth curls
into a perfect little smile
when you are dreaming.
Though I know there may be
days when stinky diapers
potty training
toddling twos
and teenage woes
may drive me to my knees –

I will always love you
always be here for you
always be your friend.
You are the sparkle in my eye
my fondest dream come true.
You have changed my way of
living, thinking, feeling, reacting.
Yes, that first hug my arms
embraced around you
bound me to you forever.
I will always treasure you,
my child.
You are God's priceless gift to me.

Psalm 139:13 *For you formed my inward parts; you knitted me in my mother's womb. I praise you, for I am fearfully and wonderfully made. Wonderful are your works; my soul know it very well.*

A Father Like You

Thank you, Father,
for a father
who instructs without
provoking the children to wrath.
For his tender concern
over a young boy's
broken truck
or a little girl's
broken heart.
For the great love and pride
he shows in them
when someone asks,
"Are all those yours?"
For patience
when he explains
over and over again
not to leave his tools
in the yard
or a bike in the rain.
Thank you, Father,
for a father
from whom they are learning
what kind of a Father
You are to us.

Proverbs 17:6 *Grandchildren are the crown of old men, and the glory of sons is their fathers. (NAS)*

I Saw the Sunrise

This morning while eating my breakfast,
My wee little daughter of three
Looked across the room, out the window,
And let out a squeal of glee.

"Look, Mommy, look!" she demanded.
"Looket, out there at the sky!"
I glanced, then gazed, then I focused
On the glorious feast to my eyes!

We went to the window together
And there for the next little while
I drank in the love in her laughter
As each color brought new joy and smiles.

I thought as I stood there enthralled
In the joy of her discovery
What splendor and radiance Your sunrise
On my sinful soul brought to me.

My soul was lying in stillness,
The darkness of sin had me bound,
Till the glorious light of the Gospel
Beamed Your love to me all around.

Thank you, Father, this morning
For so many blessings I know.
For the joy of a sunrise with Kristie,
And the sunlight You brought to my soul!

John 8:12 *Again he spoke to them saying, 'I am the light of the world. Whoever follows me will not walk in darkness but will have the light of life.'*

Thank You for My Little Ones

Thank You for my little ones' hugs,
The "pay attention to me now, Mom" tugs,
And even Tommy's gift of bugs.
Thank You for my little ones' hugs.

Thank You for my little ones' sighs,
Their "I need a band aid on it!" cries,
And especially squeals of surprise!
Thank You for my little ones' sighs.

Thank You for my little ones' prayers,
The "Jesus Loves Me" songs they share,
For sweet dependence on Your care!
Thank You for my little ones' prayers.

Luke 18:16 *But Jesus called them to him, saying, 'Let the children come to me, and do not hinder them, for to such belongs the Kingdom of God.'*

Matthew

Strong
tender
volatile
loving
precariously standing
somewhere between
the boy
and the man.
Sometimes it is hard
for a mother
to know which one she is
addressing.
Father,
help me
let go
of childhood demands.
He is beyond the training years,
and he resents my
attempt to force him back
into that mold.
He is in the becoming years
expanding mind, body, soul, spirit
exploring
expressing with words, music
song.
He is his own person
independent
no longer in need
of a trainer
but a guide.
Father, help me not pull
so much for my way
as Yours.
Help me learn to
adjust

to the careful exchanges
of Motherhood.

Proverbs 22:6 *Train up a child in the way he should go; even when he is old he will not depart from it.*

Special Days/Occasions

The Risen Lord

The clouds of Calvary hang low
and bitter anguish grips the soul
of God's sinless sacrifice.

The veil is rent, the Savior cries,
Embodied Grace for mankind dies
and followers deny.

Pale mourners come with spices sweet
intending to anoint the feet
of Christ, the crucified.

As angels meet the mourners there
a cry rips through the sorrowed air,
"He is alive again!"

In jubilant retreat, some flee,
while others step inside to see
the empty tomb;

And firm denial dies to doubt
as life revived in faith cries out,
"My Savior and my God!"

The clouds of Easter still hang low
when multitudes refuse to know
their great eternal need.

And followers of Christ still cry
when those in unbelief deny
The Risen Lord.

Matthew 28:1 *Now after the Sabbath, toward the dawn of the first day of the week,
Mary Magdalene and the other Mary went to see the tomb.*

Resurrection Morning

There was only darkness
that deathful day.
The clamor of nails banging,
thieves dying,
and angry shouts of "crucify"
still rang in their ears.
A knock at the door
was barely noticed – then,
trembling
they feared a Roman guard –
the Jews?
It was Mary
face anguished
so hysterical with grief
she could barely talk
out of breath from
running, they surmised.
From whom?
Calm down.
What news have you of our
arrest?
An empty tomb?
They took Him?
Where?
Mary, are you certain?
His body – gone?

Running now they forget
their trembling
stretching out the ache of
mourning
to accommodate their
stride of terrorized hope.
Could He be – alive?
Coming to the tomb
they clasp hands

briefly squeezing
as if to make sure
they themselves are still
alive.

The stone HAS been rolled away.
One stoops to peer inside
while the other enters
boldly bounding in
and handles empty clothes of
death
still warm.

They wander back to hiding
now in silence.
Careful steps cadence the
phrase
"I'll rise again.
I'll rise again."
Was this the hope He spoke of?
Could Jesus be
raised from the dead?
Unspoken questions
flash between their glances.

Back inside
their shackled room
they whisper details
of the empty tomb.
Suddenly
among them stands
the Risen Lord
fresh from the grave of victory
and all the doubt of
yesterday
shock
flash of fear
melts into

Hope and
wild rejoicing –
HE IS ALIVE!

John 20

Easter Morn

Three nights now have passed
since they crowned Him
with the thorns from the
curse of the ground.

Three nights I've spent
sleepless and sorrowing
at the thought of His body
brought down...

Three nights I have trembled
and wondered
where the hope of tomorrow
now lies.

Three nights now have marked
the duration
of my mournful and
heartbroken cries...

But it's morning the third day.

The air in the garden
this morning
is misty and speckled with dawn,

But coming to see
my Lord Jesus
I find that His body
is gone.

Oh, where? Tell me where
have you laid Him?
Tell me, where have they
taken my Lord?

Oh, please, sir,
passing there in the garden,
tell me, where have they
taken my Lord?

What word do I hear?

No one else speaks my name
like the Master
with a love
that erases all time.

With a joy
that eclipses all sorrow
and a hope
that's eternally mine!

My own name is like
flowering beauty
in the mouth of my Savior,
my Friend.

As I turn quickly now,
I behold Him.
He is risen
and living again!

Oh, yes, Lord!
I will run on to tell them!
I have seen You myself
and I know

That You truly have risen
from death and the grave,
I'll run quickly and tell them
I'll go!

Oh, Glorious news –

stop your crying!
Let your tears of defeat
find their end!

For the Savior of Glory
has risen!
He is reigning
triumphant again!

Run into the streets
tell the wounded –
tell the bleeding,
the dying, the lame –

That we are the reason
He went to the cross
and ascended
triumphant again!

Tell the sorrowing heart,
Hope is living!
Tell the wandering soul
to come home!

For the King of Salvation
is Risen!
And is reigning in grace
on His throne!!

John 20

My Gift to the King of Eternity

The drummer boy asked, Lord, I ask, too,
What possible gift can I bring to You?
A King who hung upon a tree
desiring all humanity
to come behold the Lamb of God,
Eternal King whose blood was shed
that, undeserving as I am,
would take hold of Your nail-scarred hand
and walk with You and live and grow
in grace so all the world will know
Your name, Your gift to all mankind
the end of death, the battle won!
To do this through the Spirit's power
To walk in Truth through every hour
To love as I have been loved, too.
Then someday, Lord, I'll look like You.

I wonder what my world will see
today, tomorrow, through eternity when they look at me...
Tell me, Father, do I look like You?
Are these yet Your hands; do my feet go
wherever the Father tells me to
as You did?
Oh, Father, do I have Your heart?
Do I yet love without a part reserved for me?
Dear Father, in Your master plan
You will not leave me as I am,
but one day when You look at me
the King of all Eternity will be reflected in what You see.

Today, Lord, may I give You more
than I have given You before.
May every fiber of me be
reflecting Your love outwardly
as I am loving You within.
Oh, Father, may my world then

see You when they look at me.
This my gift to the King of eternity.

1 Corinthians 13:12 *For now we see in a mirror dimly, but then face to face. Now I know in part; then I shall know fully, even as I have been fully known.*

Ornaments of Grace

Father,
it is the season of Your birth.
We celebrate with carols and bells,
tinsel and ribbon,
shopping and crowds and noise and
too much money spent
on gifts that have
nothing whatsoever to do with You.

Cut tree farms grow rootlessly on every corner
and countless people plod along
obediently matching cadence
with the frenzied expectations
of the season.
Tempers mount and nerves fray
as each calendar December day
is penciled in with must-do festivities,
responsibilities of Christmas.

Every year we seem to stretch the Christmas clock
a few more days or weeks or months ahead –
maybe then there will be enough time.
But typically we fall wearily into the
eve of Christmas pew
and, candles lit, are once again reminded
that Your coming had nothing to do
with all our tinsel-ridden expectations of Christmas Day.

What exactly are we trying to accomplish, Lord?

Do we think we will soon replicate the sky-exploding star
the angelic multitude announcement of Your birth
to sleepy startled shepherds in a field?
You came, Lord, Light of the World
Blazing a redemptive trail
from heavenly throne

to assume temporary residence in the
land of Your earthly footstool!
What sacrifice of love
one day apart from Your Glory laid aside
was there portrayed
on the day of Your virgin birth!
So easily the enemy
draws our gaze effortlessly
from You to empty pursuit of material more –
Especially at Christmas.

Oh Father,
Help us find our way back
to the stable and the star
the cradle and the cross.
Guide us through this
sin-darkened world
to souls still asleep in a field of night.
With Your Righteous Right Hand, Lord,
place each of us as
Ornaments of Your Grace
on the trees of our personal fields of influence.
May we shine with Your love
in a world filled with night
and light the way to You.

Luke 2:11 *For unto you is born this day in the City of David a Savior, Who is Christ the Lord.*

I Will Praise You in the Hallway

I will praise you in the hallway
I will praise you in the storm
I will praise you in the darkness
I will praise you when I'm worn.
When the last ounce of my efforts
Cease to bring about relief
I will praise you as The Great I Am.
Lord, help my unbelief.

I will praise you when with ill intent
Evil marks my door.
When it creeps in through the windows
And it oozes through the floor.
I will praise you when at last I fall
Exhausted in a heap.
I will praise you as my Sovereign King
You hold my soul—you keep.

I will praise you when the water pots
Are heavy on my neck
And the wilderness I travel in
Has not relented yet.
I will praise you when all hope seems lost
And every ocean drained.
I will praise you still Water of Life
And thirst for you again.

I will praise you in the gladness
Of an unexpected gift.
When, just in time, an angel comes
To give my soul a lift.
I will praise you when the moments
Of my laughter quiet fall.
I will praise you as my Comforter
And trust you with it all.

I will praise you in the openness
Of newness and delight.
I will see you in creation-
A Blue Heron taking flight-
I will follow you with hope
And I will follow you to more
I will praise you, Resurrected One
I'll dance with you—I'll soar!

Philippians 4:4 *Rejoice in the Lord always; again I will say rejoice.*

1 Thessalonians 5:16 *Rejoice always.*

Postlude

Eighteen years after the abuse that began the *Psalms* writings, deep in the throes of depression, and again with serious consideration of suicide, I sought a Christian counselor. Due to my devastating experience with a religious figure, I was afraid to confide in anyone religious and/or connected with a church locally. I expanded my search options. I found a clinic in Little Rock, AR linked to a nationally reputable name and tentatively trusted my disintegrating heart and life to that clinic and to its Dr. Rice.

My first forty-five minute appointment with him lasted more than an hour. After some casual niceties of introduction, his instruction was simple – "Just start wherever you want to start." With timidity and great emotional distance, I began, "I was born…" walking him through what little I understood of my story at that time. I told him about my childhood, chaotic home life, difficult adolescence, and what seemed to me the most devastating betrayal of all— the spiritual, psychological and sexual abuse I experienced at the hands of a religious leader. I had no tears as I spoke. No emotion laced my voice. I felt numb and dead inside. I spit out the facts of my life as if reporting what had happened to someone long dead. Although my perspective assigned all blame to me—particularly the most recent abuse—when I looked from the window out of which I had been staring to the face of the good doctor, he was leaning forward in his chair, elbows on the desk between us and, with an incredulous expression on his face, startled me when he spoke. "Do you know that man should have gone to prison for what he did to you?" I could not believe his words… "Really? Really? You mean…it…wasn't my fault?"

"No, my dear woman. It was definitely not your fault!"

The relief I experienced—the freedom I embraced—on that day cannot be overstated. For the next two years I drove weekly to see Dr. Rice and, with the help of his expert mental health care, I very slowly began my journey back to life. Longings to learn also stirred with the opening of the kind doctor's invitation to life—I started to dream again.

When my children were in elementary school, my hunger to learn was piqued as I listened to them read and helped with their homework. But I was extremely intimidated by their teachers and found it difficult to converse with them because I felt so inferior. Parent/teacher conferences were torture, and I often left the school in tears—not because my children received bad reports, quite the contrary—because I was so painfully sure I was an incurable idiot.

At the same time I was counseling with Dr. Rice, God was dealing with me about the shackles that bound me to the lie that I could not learn, and a long-buried desire ignited. With a great deal of fear and uncertainty, but with the determination to follow hard after God, I enrolled in a non-college credit basic math course at the local state technical institute just to get over my fear of math. That was my goal. Much to my surprise, I got an A! I sincerely thought that grade was a fluke so I took another step and enrolled in intermediate math—another non-college credit course—and earned another A. I was thrilled, and the success I felt fueled my determination to continue my pursuit of knowledge. I began to dream of a college education. I knew I wanted to study counseling and psychology. I also knew I wanted to learn the disciplines from a Christian perspective. I added a creative writing class to my college credit courses and boldly enrolled in college algebra. Two more A's. I was ecstatic! Maybe my mother was wrong – maybe I *could* learn.

Fueled by success and desire, I applied and was accepted at Crichton College – a local Christian liberal arts college – and dove in with all I had. I worked hard to maintain my GPA and received tuition assistance by being on the Dean's List every semester I attended. I participated in extracurricular activities: I was cast as Yenchna the vendor in the Neil Simon's play *Fools* and served as editor of the college newsletter. My three children, who also were all now in college, cheered me on, as did my husband. Two of my children transferred from the University of Memphis to Crichton College during the time I was a student there. We would often meet after class or sit together in chapel. I sometimes felt the need to pinch myself to see if I was really alive. I could not believe my life. As I walked across the stage December 1997, to receive my Bachelor of Science degree in Psychology – Summa Cum Laude – I twirled! My mother, father, sister, husband, children, and friends were all in the audience cheering me on. I was 47-years-old.

Once I tasted the thrill of learning, I hungered for more. God kept opening doors for me, and I kept walking through them. I applied and was accepted at the University of Memphis where I earned Masters and Education Specialist degrees in School Psychology. During my time at U of M, I was amazed to see how much God was using my early childhood experiences to inform my learning and became so aware of God's goodness to redeem my story.

I applied and was accepted into the doctoral program for Counselor Education and Supervision at the University of Mississippi. The college was 75 miles from our home near Memphis; close enough to make the trek two or three times a week for evening classes. My mother, children, husband, and friends attended my hooding and graduation ceremonies in May 2004, when I rightfully added the letters Ph.D. to the end of my name.

Throughout my years in college, I periodically sent Dr. Rice cards to let him know where I was on my educational journey. On the day I received my Ph.D., Dr. Rice called to congratulate me. God's redemption and reconciliation are so sweet.

For the 10 years I walked through the educational doors God opened for me, my husband was my biggest fan and a vital part of my success. Our relationship was challenged, stretched and deepened as we navigated the journey together. I had been a stay-at-home mom for most of our marriage. He came from a generation that believed a woman's place was in the home. But we met the challenge of this totally new territory with faith and a willingness to follow God's lead.

Another door swung open for me when, in 2006, I became a colleague of my former instructors and professors at Crichton College. In the years that followed, I was promoted to Associate Professor, helped launch Crichton's first master's program in counseling, became Chair of the Department of Behavioral Sciences and received the "Women History Maker Award for Excellence in Education" (2012) – an honor procured through nomination and election by my peers.

Part of my journey at Crichton College involved walking with my colleagues and students through the transition from a not-for-profit institution to a for-profit institution when Crichton College was bought by Significant Psychology LLC and became Victory University (2011).

It was also during my time at Crichton College that my husband was diagnosed with his debilitating illness. His 44-year career as an AT&T employee came to an end when he was told he had to retire for medical reasons. It became very clear to us that, more than 10 years prior when I didn't think I could learn, and we had no idea I would need to be the provider for our family, God knew, led me to Dr. Rice, called me to face my fears and invited me to pursue higher education. He is such a faithful provider.

The most recent chapter in my professional journey is no less a part of God's redemptive work. At Victory University I learned a great deal about myself as a leader. It is also a place where I was confronted with my commitment to honest and ethical business practice. My husband and I prayed and asked God to move us to east Tennessee for over two years for a number of reasons, not the least of which being we have always loved this end of the state. It is also where our daughter, son-in-law, and two of our three grandchildren reside. Although I submitted resumes to entities in Knoxville and Chattanooga, no offers ensued.

One particularly difficult day at Victory, I had what amounts to an adult temper fit before God. I complained loudly (in the privacy of my office) and asked Him why He had not answered our prayers to move. The next day, I lay prostrate before Him on my office floor and asked Him to forgive my rant, vowing to follow Him *wherever* He might lead – even if that meant staying right where I was. My motto became, "Until the next door opens, I will praise You in the hallway." A poem about this profound experience of faith is included in the "Reorientation" section of *Psalms*.

During my lunch hour that same afternoon, as I was scrolling through job postings on HigherEd.com, I spotted a listing for a Counselor Educator at Milligan College. I had never heard of Milligan College or the town in which it was located, but quickly identified its location in East Tennessee. As I read through the job listing, I was amazed to note that I fit the qualifications of the position perfectly—I had the credentials and experience for every one that was listed. I went home that Friday evening, showed the posting to my husband, and we agreed I would submit an application the next day. That was in late April 2013. The position began August 15, 2013.

The Milligan people with whom I interacted through email, Skype interview, and a campus visit made a great impression on me. The beauty of the area was stunning, and the campus warm and inviting. I remember walking out of the campus theatre building and seeing, "*In the beginning was the Word...*" written on a large stone. That is my husband's favorite scripture. Everything I experienced during that visit seemed to confirm that God was opening a door for me at Milligan. And, indeed, He did. In the whirlwind of necessary activity that followed my campus visit, I experienced the beauty of what it means to be part of the Milligan community. God further confirmed that His hand led me to Milligan when, in March 2014, Victory University announced that they were closing and my Victory colleagues were suddenly without jobs.

The current chapter of my spiritual journey is rich in relationship and opportunity to learn more of my story and to grow more in love with Jesus. Open Hearts Ministry and Red Tent Living are vital parts of my story. Without the healing journey I have known through my association with these ministries, along with the advanced training I've received in trauma and abuse at The Allender Center, the writings of Dan Allender and others, my experiences at Recovery Week, the love and teaching ministry of a good and godly pastor (Richard Hipps) and loving church family (Trinity Baptist in Memphis), I would not be where I am today. God has consistently directed me through the good men and women who have listened to my story, helped me see beauty in the ashes, sat with me, cried with me, grieved with me, encouraged my faith, helped me fall more in love with Jesus and consistently called me to more.

God wastes nothing. He redeems, reconciles, and renews. I pray that as you continue to read the entries in this little book, you will hear the voice of God calling you to His precious, healing side. You do not have to journey alone. There are Journey Groups (a function of Open Hearts Ministry) in many cities throughout the United States and even internationally where you can begin to uncover more of your story and walk into it with people who will be with you, support you, and help you grieve. There are books and conferences listed in the index that will encourage your discoveries and equip your search—and there are good pastors and congregations where you can plant your life in order to serve the King and the Kingdom of God. I pray you will avail yourself of these wonderful resources.

It has been said that one of the greatest and most terrifying words to a survivor of childhood sexual abuse is *hope*. We have hoped for so much only to know repeated disappointment. But that is not the end of the story. Where there is hope, there is life, there is newness, there is opportunity, and there is more.

Remember that nagging nursery rhyme–HORRID? I rewrote it...
There once was a girl who lived in a world
Filled with evil and hatred and strife.
Her Beloved then came, took all of her shame
And is redeeming her one wild and beautiful life!

I am so thankful to those who continually call me to more. I echo their voices here, now, to you. There is a place for you at the Table of Life. Come and dine.

With love and appreciation to all who have so faithfully built into my life,
Christine

Resources and Works Cited

Allender, D. (2016). *Healing the wounded heart: The heartache of sexual abuse and the hope of transformation.* Grand Rapids, MI: Baker Books.

Allender, D. (2006). *Leading with a limp: Turning your struggles into strengths.* Colorado Springs, CO: WaterBrook Press.

Allender, D. (1999). *The healing path: How the hurts in your past can lead you to a more abundant life.* New York, NY: WaterBrook Press.

Allender, D. (1990). *The wounded heart: Hope for adult victims of childhood sexual abuse.* Colorado Springs, CO: Navpress.

Allender, D. (2005). *To be told: God invites you to coauthor your future.* Colorado Springs, CO: WaterBrook Press.

Bateman, L. (1985). *God's crippled children: Hope for emotionally hurting Christians.* Dallas, TX: Lana Bateman.

Cohen, J.A., Mannarino, A.P., & Deblinger, E. (2006). *Treating trauma and traumatic grief in children and adolescents.* New York, NY: Guilford Press.

Gibbons, K. (1990). *Ellen Foster.* New York: Vintage Books: A Division of Random House, Inc. (pg. 76).

Herman, J. (1997). *Trauma and recovery: The aftermath of violence—from domestic abuse to political terror.* New York, NY: BasicBooks.

Johnson, K. (1998). *Trauma in the lives of children: Crisis and stress management techniques for counselors, teachers, and other professionals.* Alameda, CA: HunterHouse.

Jones, S. (2009). *Trauma & grace: Theology in a ruptured world.* Louisville, KY: Westminster John Knox Press.

Langberg, D.M. (1999). *On the threshold of hope: Opening the door to healing for survivors of sexual abuse.* Carol Stream, IL: Tyndale House Publishers, Inc.

Russell, D.E.H. (1999). *The secret trauma: Incest in the lives of girls and women* (2nd ed.). New York, NY: BasicBooks.

Van der Kolk, B.A., McFarlane, A.C., & Weisaeth, L. (Eds.). (2007). *Traumatic stress: The effects of overwhelming experience on mind, body, and society.* New York, NY: The Guilford Press.

Wardle, T. (2007). *Strong winds & crashing waves: Meeting Jesus in the memories of traumatic events.* Abilene, TX: Leafwood Publishers.

Open Hearts Ministry
web: ohmin.org

You can contact Open Hearts for information on Journey Groups in your area.

The Allender Center website has a plethora of offerings/resources (i.e., a list of conferences; speaking engagements; Recovery Weeks; advanced training in trauma and abuse for lay workers and professional counselors and more). www.theallendercenter.org

Psalms Of My Heart

CPSIA information can be obtained
at www.ICGtesting.com
Printed in the USA
LVHW080311221022
731103LV00001B/1